THIS GUN'S FOR HIRE

A Look inside the Mind of a Street Cop

Terrence Howard

iUniverse, Inc.
Bloomington

THIS GUN'S FOR HIRE
A LOOK INSIDE THE MIND OF A STREET COP

iUniverse books may be ordered through booksellers or by contacting:

iUniverse
1663 Liberty Drive
Bloomington, IN 47403
www.iuniverse.com
1-800-Authors (1-800-288-4677)

ISBN: 978-1-4759-2852-5 (sc)
ISBN: 978-1-4759-2854-9 (hc)
ISBN: 978-1-4759-2853-2 (ebk)

Printed in the United States of America

iUniverse rev. date: 06/08/2012

CONTENTS

DEDICATION

On April 16, 2007, I began writing this book. On that day, I had just finished working the midnight shift and was about to head to the bar for a cocktail. It was the 16th day of the month and that meant one thing on the Chicago Police Dept. It's payday. I looked at my paycheck and it looked different. That's when I discovered that $1,385.00 had been deducted from my pay for a federal tax levy. In 2004, my mother passed away and she left me some money in her will. It appeared that the IRS felt that my mother left some money for them too, so they took their share from me. I was totally depressed and feeling sorry for myself. That is until I drove home and turned on the television.

The mass murder of the students of Virginia Tech. University was on every channel. I couldn't believe what I was hearing. A psychopath was taking the lives of young, innocent college students, full of promise and in the prime of their lives. I stopped feeling sorry for myself and my heart went out to those students and teachers killed, those that survived, the parents that lost a child and the university. I broke a cardinal rule. I took their murders personal.

After the shooting ended and the killer killed himself, the media came in to interview the survivors. What I saw was unbelievable. The students interviewed showed so much courage, composure and class that I was truly touched. There was no malice in their hearts. Not even toward the shooter. Only that they would recover from this tragedy and carry on with their lives. The man who committed that horrible act failed in his mission. The students were devastated, but they were not destroyed. They came together as a family and showed the world how to handle adversity.

In my life, I have been inspired by great athletes and jazz musicians. April 16, 2007, and the subsequent days after that tragedy, I was inspired by the students of Virginia Tech University and I dedicate this book to them. Dr. Martin Luther King Jr. said that the true test of a man is not how he handles the times of comfort and calm. The true test is how he handles the bad times and sustains the vicious blows. Those students passed the test.

ACKNOWLEDGMENTS

To my mother, Claudia C Howard. Ma passed away in 2004, but not before she instilled in me the values that have lasted me a lifetime. My mother also planted the seed. She convinced me to take the police exam. Whenever I listened to my mother, I never went wrong. I love you Ma. I miss having you here with me.

For a boy to become a man, he needs a good model of a man to look up to. I was lucky to have two men in my life. To my father, Lige W Howard and my high school orchestra director, Dr. Joseph L Miller, I owe a lot. Those men showed me that when you do anything in life, you do it right. Dr. Miller used a drum stick against my head and my father used an extension cord against my behind. I got the message.

To my wife Sandra, who was there from the beginning. She didn't want me to take the job. She thought it was too dangerous. She accepted it with time. Sandra will always be my first, my last, and my only wife. To our children: Jerome, Tyrone, Antoinette and Terrence Jr. It was for you guys and your mother that I worked so hard. To the family I gained through my marriage. They took me in and made me feel like family too.

To my aunts, uncles, cousins, niece and nephew (who I didn't spend near enough time with over the years). I can only say that I thought of you all in my prayers. Life in general is hard enough. When you add alcoholism and policing to the mix, it's a bad combination. I wish I'd spent more time with my family than I spent with Budweiser, Jack Daniels and Crown Royal.

To the men and women of the Chicago Police Department. The veteran officers that showed me the ropes. The officers that joined the force with me. We learned the game together. The rookies that came along toward the end of the journey. I can't name them all. They know who they are.

Five officers had a major impact on my career. My field training officer Donald Fanelli. (You did good Don. You trained me right.) Herbert E Bailey Jr. (My mentor, teacher and measuring stick. R.I.P. HB.) Fredrick King. (Baseball coach to the future stars. Freddie never ate, slept, or stopped writing tickets. Except to go shopping.) John Williams Jr. (The younger brother I handpicked to train. "Po' Pimp" made the cut.) Michael Casey. (The coolest "white dude" I ever partnered with.) I have to give a shout out to "my boys." Charlie Black, Heavy D, Dave "Po' Boy" Hill, "Tony Tony" Randle, Tony "A little coke: a lot of rum" Finney (R.I.P.) and Spiderman.

When you lose one brother, it's hard to fill that void. I lost my three brothers in 10 years. To my brothers: Kenneth, Rodney and Everett Howard. It was the memory of them that kept me going on. On the many days I didn't want to go on anymore. I wanted to be with my brothers.

INTRODUCTION

Never in my dreams did I ever see myself joining a police department. In 1986, I didn't know much about the police. I did know this. The police were a group of people I didn't want around me and I didn't want to be around them. When I did join the force, 24 years of my life were invested in a single motto: "We Serve And Protect." As the years passed, the motto changed. Less serve and protect and more observe and collect. The profession really became a part of my identity. I was committed to the people I served (the public) and the people I worked with (my fellow officers).

Once on the force, I looked, listened and learned from some of the best in the business. I studied their styles and used a little of all styles to create my own. At the same time, I studied the people on the streets. In order to beat an opponent, you need to know their strengths and their weaknesses. This is a serious game. In law enforcement, it's winner takes all. The price police officers might pay if they lose the game could be their lives.

I never intended to write a book. This began as a letter to the editor of the Chicago Sun Times. This book had been growing inside my head for 21 years. That's how long I had been on the police force when I started writing the book. That's how long I'd been listening to my friends trying to tell me how to be "The Police." Friends that don't know what the hell they're talking about. That's how long I'd been listening to people in the media doing talk shows and writing newspaper articles with all their Monday morning quarterbacking nonsense. More people that don't have a clue. I decided to try and give an actual, factual account of who, what, when, where, why, and how police officers come into being what they ultimately become.

This story is based on my 24 years of service on the streets of Chicago. This book will take a very honest look at a very dangerous occupation. Being on the front line: a first responder to murders, stabbings, armed robberies, rape, fatal car crashes, suicides and drive-by shootings ain't like watching it on the 10 o'clock news. The news isn't all bad. The ugly side is just a part of it. A cop has an exciting, unpredictable job that is never the same from day to day.

Through the police department, I was able to meet the rich and the famous. I didn't have to wait in line to meet them either. The greatest reward from the job is an officer gets to (sometimes) right what's wrong in the world. To be able to help someone that can't help himself gives one a good feeling. The police may not be the most revered group of people you may think of. Think about this. What would this crazy world be like with no policemen?

So, sit back and relax while I tell you my story through my own experience. My intention is not to try and write the Great American Novel. My intent is to give the reader of this book an inside look into the mind of street cops who do it for real. This police life is for real. This ain't no god damn movie! Real guns. Real bullets. Real blood. No director sitting in a chair shouting "Cut" or "Action." Get shot in those streets and guess what? You bleed.

I want to apologize in advance for the use of profanity in telling this tale. I've heard it said that you shouldn't have to use profanity to make your point. That might be true in Beverly Hills. In Chicago, that's straight bullshit. On the streets of Chicago, profanity is the only language some people understand. Officer "Friendly" works with some people. Officer "I will fuck you up" works with others. As I have told many a rookie cop, I'll tell you, the reader. Come with me if you want to live. I'm about to make the police out of you.

(A Note Concerning Gender. Throughout my book, I referred to police officers in the male gender. This is not to dismiss the many fine and dedicated policewomen that I have had the honor of serving with on the Chicago Police Department. So, when you see "he" or "him," it also applies to "she" or "her.")

DISCLAIMER

This book is a work of nonfiction based totally on the author's personal experience. It is not a "how-to-do-it" manual. At no time does the author suggest or advise that the reader of this book attempt to duplicate the work style or work ethic of the author. In fact, the author strongly urges the reader not to following in his footsteps. Law enforcement officers are governed by federal and state laws, rules and regulations and department guidelines. These should be the only motivating factors for any police officer's actions. Not something that he read in my book.

During my tenure, a police officer was held to a high standard. A police officer today is held to an even higher standard. Failure to acknowledge this fact can cost an officer his career, his freedom and his life savings. Always, always think like a police officer. You will be tried and convicted as a police officer in a court of law or in front of a police review board.

CHAPTER 1

THE FORTY COMMANDMENTS

The Bible tells the story of the Ten Commandments. A police officer must battle gangs, handguns, assault weapons, murderers, armed violence, rapist, crack heads, heroin addicts, politicians seeking re-election, public opinion, civil litigation, community activist, the Internal Affairs Division, the Police Review Board and the video camera. Moses only had to fight Pharaoh. Who did Moses call when he needed back up? God. Moses couldn't lose. When you have more opponents, you'll need more commandments.

Police work is just like anything else you learn in life. Start with the basics and learn as you go. Certain tactics an officer will learn from the veterans that train him and others he will learn through personal experience. Shit happens fast on the streets. A police officer needs to have a game plan drawn up ahead of time. This ain't no dress rehearsal. This is real life.

These Forty Commandments are the "golden rules" for the police officer. The officer on the street needs to learn them all by memory. Learn them all and he might win the game. Ignore them and he's on his own. Good luck.

1. Nobody(I do mean nobody!!) wants a police officer around them until they need a police officer around them.
2. On the streets, he must always know his location. If he doesn't know where he's at, how can he get help to arrive if he needs help?
3. The police radio is what makes a police officer "The Police." Not his badge, his uniform or his gun.
4. Wherever he takes his gun, take his baton too. It's better to have it and don't need it than to need it and don't have it. He can't beat everybody with his fist and he can't shoot everybody with his gun.
5. Drive slow and think fast. Hurry up and slow down.
6. The public doesn't have a problem with gambling as long as they are gambling with someone else's life. Your life, officer.
7. When he checks prisoners for weapons, check for all their weapons.
8. Take his job serious. Don't take it personal.
9. If he stops drivers for traffic violations, he should give them a ticket or a lecture. Don't give both. If he does, he might hear this: "Officer, just write me my ticket and shut the fuck up!"
10. The public must take all of the police service or they shouldn't take any of it. If they don't want the police to write them tickets, they shouldn't call 911 when someone is stealing their car.
11. Stay alert and he'll stay alive.
12. The risk he takes should never outweigh the reward.
13. Be a hero. But, only by accident.
14. When a police officer checks off at the end of his tour of duty, check off with his life. The hell with how many tickets he wrote.

15. There's a difference between what he thinks, what he knows, and what he can prove. If he can't prove it, forget it. Leave it alone.
16. The police department is not a family. It's a business. An officer is welcome only as long as he proves to be an asset to the company. When he becomes a liability, he has to go.
17. Listen to what the public tells him. Then, try to figure out what it is they're not telling him. Trust me, that's what he really wants to know.
18. An officer doesn't get paid on commission. Write ten tickets or get shot two times. He still gets the same pay.
19. Come to work to make money, not to make friends.
20. An understanding last longer than fear.
21. Just because "it" ain't happened in the last 10 years doesn't mean "it" won't happen in the next 10 minutes. What is "it?" He never knows.
22. A policeman can not be friends with people he has to "police."
23. The right tools make his job easy. Use them. Police officers don't search abandoned buildings. Police canine units do.
24. He should look before he leaps.
25. It's better to be judged by 12 than carried to his grave by 6.
26. When off-duty, avoid the on-duty police. When on-duty, avoid the off-duty police. Off-duty police officers will make him want to kill them.
27. If he doesn't know what he's doing, ask someone that does know. There is no shame in asking for help. (Note: On the CPD, ask Officer Virginia Johnston.)
28. Everybody wants to go to heaven. Nobody wants to die.

29. If the public wants him to make them a hamburger, they shouldn't complain about how he treats the cow.
30. He should forget about Rodney King. He didn't beat him up.
31. His job title is Policeman. Not Superman, Spider Man or Aqua Man. He's not faster than a speeding bullet nor is he able to leap tall buildings in a single bound. He can't spin a web any size, catching thieves just like flies. And, he don't get wet.
32. Beware of what he writes on police reports, what he says on police audio tapes and what he does on police video tapes. Once he writes it, says it, or gets caught on tape doing it, he can't undo it.
33. Always think like a police officer because he will be tried and convicted as a police officer in a court of law.
34. A police officer can do whatever he wants to do. Until he gets caught.
35. Try to hurt him and he's gonna do whatever he has to do to stop you. He won't care what it looks like on the 6 o'clock news.
36. He will never walk into a fighting crowd of people. He can't see in front of him and behind him at the same time.
37. Women carry weapons too. Keep his eyes on her hands, not her ass.
38. He doesn't win a street fight on the street. He wins it in the gym. Same with a shoot-out. He wins it at the gun range.
39. People will gladly accept their rewards in life, but not their punishment.
40. There can never (I do mean never!!) be too many police officers at the scene of anything. There can be too few.

CHAPTER 2

The Model Police Officer

There are three models. They are assembled in the police academy. After the recruits are trained and sworn in, they leave the academy and are assigned to a district or precinct where more modifications are made. The community they train in and the veterans that train them will become the recruit's foundation. Kind of like the caterpillar stage in a butterfly's development. What develops when the rookies comes out of the cocoon will be one of three models. They will become either: 1. A Police Officer (nonactive). 2. The Police (reactive). 3. The Real Police (proactive). Warning! There is one other kind of cop.

A Police Officer

A Police Officer applied for the job, his application for hire was accepted, he took and passed the entrance exam, entered the police academy and stayed out of trouble. In the academy, he passed all the required testing, became state certified, was sworn in and graduated. Upon graduation, he was sent to a district, on probation, for street training. A Police Officer has an "every man for himself" approach to police work. He only does the work that he has to do. The radio calls he handles are the ones he gets assigned. If you don't call him, you don't see him. A Police Officer doesn't want to do the job. A Police Officer only wants to get paid on the 1st and the 16th of the month.

When an officer gets into a squad car with a DVD player and a stack of movies, a Play station or a Steven King novel, police work is not his main focus. A Police Officer will complain about how many jobs he gets during his tour of duty and brag about how much sleep he gets. There is a difference between sleeping on the job and coming to work to sleep. (Note: I worked the midnight shift for 17 years. Yes, I slept sometimes.) The difference was when the shit was hitting the fan, A Police Officer would sleep right through it. If the police dispatcher didn't call his radio number, no one would see him at the scene. He didn't come to work to help out. He came to work to sleep.

A Police Officer's rationale of a crime victim is, "Oh well. Shit happens." He takes no personal responsibility and will put the blame on the victim of the crime. Sometimes, he will come to work and predict that he won't do any work at all. This is dangerous thinking. A policeman never knows who it is that he's pulling over at a traffic stop or who's on the other side of the door he's knocking on. A Police Officer may have applied for the job thinking about the pay, the benefits, and the pension. The twice convicted felon who's looking at life in prison if you arrest him may be thinking you took the job to send him back to the penitentiary. A three time loser ain't got shit to lose and may see murdering a policeman as his only way out.

The young rookie is like a teenager with his first hard-on. He's got it and can't wait to use it. Like a teenager, the rookie really doesn't know what to do with it. Young officers want to do everything they've seen done in the cop movies or they want to police like old Uncle Pete, the retired cop, told them he used to back in the day. Bad guys die in the end of the movie. The cop lives. In real life, there is no script. Try to police like Uncle Pete and your ass might end up indicted, sued, fired or locked up. Rookies think that the veteran officers are lazy. Veteran officers don't want to score a lot of points. They just want to win the game.

Recruits, fresh out of the academy, want action. They want to receive department commendations, citations for bravery and awards for valor. There are a lot of fancy awards on the CPD. Rookies don't realize that some of those awards they won't receive until after they leave the intensive care unit. The best way to get a rookie's attention is to ask him, "What were you doing 10-15 years ago today? You were in grade school." Veterans let them know: "I was doing the same thing that I'm doing now, rookie." The good news for a recruit is the job is new and exciting. The bad news? The feeling doesn't last long. A few years on the force and he learns it's just a job.

Rookies that get assigned to work with A Police Officer caught a bad break. The rookies doesn't know anything and A Police Officer doesn't want to do anything. If they spends their probation period on the streets avoiding police work, what happens when the C/O says that they're not on probation anymore? The C/O puts them in a car, alone, and tells them, "Go to work."

The young officer is in trouble now because all he learned from A Police Officer was how to duck and dodge police work. Now, the rookie cop is supposed to know what he's doing on the streets and he doesn't know. No one took the time to show him.

(On a personal note: I didn't look forward to working with rookies late in my career. Oh, what the hell. Someone had to train me, so now it's my turn. I never talked to my recruits about writing tickets or making arrests. I tried to accelerate their training about the only thing that was important to me. Commandment 14. All the other bullshit will come with doing time on the streets. If they wrote a report wrong, they could write it over. If they failed the sergeant's exam, they could take it again. Fail the street survival test and that's their ass.)

The Police

The Police have all the qualifications of A Police Officer. He just takes his game to a higher level. He comes to work to work. He thinks like the police and also like the criminal. Doesn't need much motivating and very little supervision. He does the job right because he applied for the job, the City of Chicago hired him and now, he has a job to do. The Police do not work recklessly or fail to use due caution. He's not foolish, but he's not the faint of heart either. The Police will show up when a fellow officer needs assistance without being called to the scene by the dispatcher. He just shows up.

In the mind of The Police: "We're all in this together." His strongest attribute is a commitment to the team effort. He believes in Commandment 40 ("I might not be your best friend but I'll be the first one to back you up"). The rationale of The Police is, "Ain't shit gonna happen on my beat while I'm out here." He takes no personal responsibility for the crime victim's situation. However, he will put the blame on the offender of the crime, not the victim. The Police understands that he can't be at all places at all times. Shit does happen and that's life. No matter how many police are on the street, innocent people will be robbed, shot and killed in a large city like Chicago.

The Police always feels: "I wish I had been there. I could have made a difference."

The Real Police

Hollywood makes movies about this police officer. The wild and the crazy. He comes at the criminal hard. Wants the toughest assignments and works in the most dangerous neighborhoods. The Real Police make the big arrest. He is the shit magnet of the police department. Shit just finds him or he is finding shit. The patrol division is too slow for him. He prefers to work in plainclothes, in gang and drug units, buying drugs from dealers and getting weapons off the street. The Real Police want to get down and dirty. Run from him and he will chase you. Fight with him and he will fight you back. And yes, he will search your car without a warrant. Damn the ACLU.

The Real Police hunt for criminals like Arnold Schwarzenegger was looking for Sarah Conners. Search, locate and terminate. He does police work because he wants to. His rationale is, "I want some shit to happen." He takes personal responsibility and will be pissed off if some shit jumps off and he misses it. The community he works in despises him without realizing that the worst your community is, the more you need him. There are some neighborhoods that A Police Officer is not the best candidate to work the area. Not the case with The Police or The Real Police. They can work anywhere.

Rookies that want to learn the job should spend some time working with The Real Police. Police Officers write case reports. The Real Police write arrest reports. Lots of them. Real Police don't waste their time writing traffic tickets. Real Police are looking for hard core criminals that steal cars, sell drugs, break in homes and rob innocent people at gunpoint. It's a catch-a-mouse vs catch-a-rat mentality. Real Police catch rats and they throw mice away.

Every recruit that successfully graduates from the police academy is A Police Officer. Every recruit that graduates is not The Police. Some are just not cut out to be The Real Police. Try though he might, a cop is gonna be what he's gonna be. Understand this fact. You can not take a donkey and turn it into a race horse.

The Crooked Police

The Crooked Cop was not assembled in the police academy. He was assembled on the streets by other crooked cops or he was a crook before he got hired. A rookie, fresh out of the academy, can earn $40-$45,000.00 a year. Within a year, that officer can be earning thousands of dollars more. More than enough money to provide for himself and his family. Why do honest policemen cross the line and turn crooked? Two reasons. Reason #1 is pressure. Reason #2 is the most common. Greed.

Some policemen have pressure placed on them to produce results. The pressure may come from the Department, City Hall, the media, the C/O, public outcry, even from their peers. Certain crimes are high profile, shockingly violent and must have closure. A happy ending is required here. When a police officer is put into a pressure cooker to produce results (or else), he may start to bend the rules to get the results he needs. ("If you want to stay in my unit officer, get me the results I need.")

Policemen assigned to gang units must make gang related arrest. Officers assigned to gun units must make gun arrest. An officer assigned to those units can not stay in the unit if he's writing parking tickets every day ("What are you? The Police or a meter maid!"). When a cop starts to fold under the pressure to produce, he may start to break the rules instead of just bending the rules. Plant drugs on suspects. Violate their civil rights. Use excessive force. Go to court and "test the lie" instead of testify.

Money is still the root of all evil. Greed is the most common denominator. Most officers who fall do so because of greed or envy. Drug dealers have lots of money, nice cars, expensive clothes, jewelry, and fine ass women. Cops see this and they envy the drug dealer. The officer is thinking, "I work everyday and I can't afford a car like that." (Note: When you envy someone, you have to envy everything about them. What about the fact that the drug dealer is looking at prison time when (not if) he get busted, the other drug dealers that want to kill him, the people in his own organization that want to kill him and take his place. Plus, he can't walk the streets without looking over his shoulder every single second of the day. Now, that's pressure.)

Drug money looks very tempting on the evening news. It looks a lot more tempting staring you in the face. No one gets more jail time than a murderer, a drug dealer or a corrupt public official. That judge on the bench is gonna give away prison time like he's giving away Halloween candy. A crooked cop is gonna do all day in jail. When the police are locking up police officers, it's only one thing. Bad news.

Anytime a police scandal is uncovered, the media plays it up. The mayor, the superintendent and the State's Attorney talk about firings and jail time for the officers involved. The truth of the matter is there is always going to be police misconduct. Every three to five years, without fail, a group of dumb ass policemen are gonna screw up. People put in a position of trust are going to violate that trust. C.E.O.'s are going to launder money from the stockholders. Teachers are going to have sex with your children and priest are too. Politicians are going to accept bribes. What are we talking about here? Public officials who make mistakes in judgment.

It may be about greed, jealousy, drug money or any number of things. The crooked police will say, "I can get away with stealing this money." Maybe once. Maybe twice. Sooner or later, he will get caught. Just like the last group of dumb ass police officers who are reading this book right now in the penitentiary.

On a Personal Note

The patrol division was always looked upon as the bottom of the barrel in the police department. The patrol division is the bottom of the barrel. All the discipline, supervision and scrutiny starts in patrol. (Note: Most of the police misconduct occurs in the specialized units where there is very little supervision.) There was one advantage to working in the patrol division and that's why I stayed in patrol. No pressure. I had no pressure to produce because I could do anything. Write traffic tickets, parking tickets, curfew citations, school absentee reports, ordinance complaints, answer the 911 calls for service and make arrest. Plus, I had my beat to patrol. I was not locked into a specific area of enforcement. I was under no pressure to arrest anyone. I made my fair share. If the offender was gone when I arrived on the scene of a call, I only had to write an accurate report and turn it over to a tactical unit, gang unit or a detective unit. The pressure to catch the offender was on them now. Not on me.

Detectives have to close cases. Gang and drug enforcement officers have to make gang and drug arrest. Sometimes, even when they don't want to. I got to pick and choose if I wanted to make an arrest for drug possession. If I found someone in possession of 40 bags of heroin and cash money, to me, you were a drug dealer and I'd lock you up. If you had a crack pipe and a dime bag of crack cocaine in your pocket, you were a crack head to me. Fuck locking you up! Why? For one, you're a drug addict and you've got enough problems. Secondly, I'm not about to waste 3 hours of my time processing a pebble of crack cocaine and a broken piece of metal pipe. I was a beat cop. I can just as well write a parking ticket. Hell, I might make that crack head smoke the crack rock in front of me and then tell him to get the hell off my beat.

I have worked with every kind of police officer over a 24 year career. I was a patrolman and my badge was the same size as the patrolman standing next to me. I did not judge my fellow officers nor did I allow them to judge me. Police officers are a funny sort. Some officers just go with the flow and others act like they've got something to prove. My own philosophy about policing was simple. If I check off at the end of my tour of duty looking the same way I looked when I came to work, that was a good night. If I looked different (a cast on my arm, going home on crutches, an ace bandage wrapped around my head, a broken jaw, etc), that was a fucked up night.

On the streets, a police officer has to sell himself to the public. He doesn't have to sell himself to other police officers. The truth about every cop will come out when the shit hits the fan. That's when he shows what he's made of. When a policeman goes running in the direction of gunshots being fired and everybody else is running in the opposite direction, he just proved that he is qualified to wear the badge.

CHAPTER 3

FIVE PEOPLE

Police officers deal with many people in a variety of situations. A bartender only wants to know one thing. "What would you like to drink?" Cops must assess the people they meet quickly. Is this person someone I need to help? Is that person someone I need to fear? How quickly he makes an assessment is critical to an officer's survival. How accurately he makes an assessment can be the difference between a policeman eating his dinner at home, in the hospital, or not eating his dinner at all.

In a better world, a police officer could treat each and every citizen in a professional and respectful manner. We don't live in a better world. We live in the real world. In the real world, an officer must speak several different languages to communicate to several different types of people. The officer never knows which type of person he's in contact with until that person starts to talk. Sometimes, the people can fool him into thinking they're something that they're not. Most often, the officer knows as soon as they open their mouth. Regardless of the color of their skin, the size of their bank account or the level of their education; all people will fall within these five groups.

1. People that want to listen

They do not deal with the police on a daily basis. Most are educated, civilized and new to this police/citizen interaction. They respect the officer as the authority. Oftentimes, they are the victim of a crime and might be a little nervous or they've committed some minor infraction while driving their car. The best news about these people? They usually have never been arrested and they're not trying to start now. People that want to listen do not want to go to jail. They just want to get this police/citizen encounter over with quickly. They don't want any trouble with the police.

People that want to listen will tell a police officer their problem and listen to the officer's answer. They may not agree with the officer, but they will listen. They may be unaware that they've committed a minor traffic violation. Ignorance of the law is not a defense. If they didn't know, it is an excuse. The police want to help people that want to listen. A policeman is much willing to listen to a citizen if the citizen will listen to the police officer. A driver that will listen will probably get the lecture instead of the ticket. Here's the proof.

Example: The soccer game

One night, I was working with Officer Mona Pierce and we got a call from police dispatch. "Noise disturbance. Midway Plaisance Park." Upon arrival, we observed about 10-15 students from the University of Chicago playing soccer in the park after park district hours. Mona and I could have wrote them all tickets if we wanted to. I got on the squad car PA and stated, "Attention. The park is closed. The park will reopen at 6 o'clock. Goodnight." With no delay, the students picked up their soccer ball, moved the nets together, left the park and went home. The moral of the story? People that listen are the people the cop on the street is looking out for. They are the sheep and the police are the sheepdogs trying to keep them safe.

2. People that need a wake up. You must get their attention

The men and women that pay an officer's salary. The taxpayers. They see the police officer as just a tool to aid them. "Do your job, officer. Just not on me." You might hear them ask a police officer, "Do you know who I am?" In society, they may be a "somebody" and feel that they are above the law. (Note: In my experience, there is one specific group that has this attribute and they've got it bad. Who you ask? White people with good jobs.)

White people with good jobs are not accustomed to the police stopping them. They feel that they're the good guys and to a certain degree, they are.

(What reasons do they have to be criminals? They have good jobs with benefits.) They are law abiding citizens. The crimes they commit will land them in traffic court or misdemeanor court. They expect the police to enforce the major crimes, not the minor ones they break. They feel the police departments of the world are to protect them from those mad dog Blacks and Hispanics that they see on the evening news.

To compare themselves to killers and rapist is unthinkable. No matter what they do, their response is usually something like: "It's no big thing. It won't happen again. Thank you, officer. Goodbye." (Translation: "Fuck off, officer!! I pay your salary!!")

Whenever I would write White people tickets, they'd appear to be in shock. "How dare you! How can you do this to me?" The law does not differentiate the penalty between White people with good jobs, with no criminal history and unemployed crack heads that run stop signs. They both get the same tickets. Here's the proof.

Example: Name this celebrity

Picture this in your mind. You see a famous, wealthy, skinny ass, blond heiress. She has a suspended driver's license and has been ordered by a judge not to drive. However, the fact that she is rich ("That's hot!") gives her the impression that she can drive a car while television cameras are taking pictures of her doing it and the judge isn't gonna do anything about it. The moral of the story? How do you get her attention? Handcuffs. When that judge put her ass in jail, he got her undivided attention.

Warning!!!!

Here's the shit list. The world would be a better place without them.

3. People that want to talk

The people from "the hood." From the streets. Being stopped by the police is nothing new to them. They don't like the police. They're uneducated, uncivilized, and ignorant. The only constitutional right they remember from the high school they dropped out of is their freedom of speech. Trust me, they are gonna talk. The one weapon they can use against the police without being arrested, beat up or killed is their mouth. People that want to talk may be crazy, but they're not stupid. They know just how far to go with the shit talking. They don't cross the line with the police. They'll talk right up to the point of arrest and then they stop talking and walk away. Sometimes, they don't walk away fast enough.

People that want to talk like to tell police officers what they need to be doing, where they need to be working, and who they need to be fucking with. They want to talk about anything and everything except what they did or what they're doing right now. People that want to talk bark loud. They don't bite. They won't put an officer in fear for his life. The officer's only fear is that they will talk him to death. Here's the proof.

Example: The basketball game

One night, I was working with my partner John and we had a radio dispatch. "Noise disturbance. Men playing basketball in Lake Meadows Park after park district hours." Upon arrival, we observed about 8 men in the park playing basketball. John and I could have wrote them all tickets if we wanted to. I got on the squad car PA and stated, "Attention. The park is closed. The park will reopen at 6 o'clock. Goodnight." Now, I know they heard what I said because I heard myself say it. What do they do? Start talking shit, to wit: ("These motherfuckers ain't got shit better to do than fuck with us!! Go find some real criminals to fuck with!! Take your punk ass on the north side and fuck with the white people!!"). Let me also mention that they kept right on playing ball. So, I light up a Kool 100, called for a few more cars to respond (I didn't want them to start running and get away) and when the extra cars arrived, we wrote all their asses tickets. The moral of the story? Policemen don't argue with people that want to talk. Policemen let their pens do the talking.

4. People that don't give a fuck

They will come right out and tell a police officer to his face, "I don't give a fuck!!" The fact that the officer is the law doesn't mean a god damn thing. "Fuck the police!!" Been in and out of jail their whole life. They smoke too much reefer and listen to way too much gangster rap music. Just a small step away from the last group on the countdown. These people don't really qualify for a killing, not just yet. They are prime candidates for a good ass whipping. (Note: If they campaign hard enough for an ass whipping, I believe they deserve to get elected. People that don't give a fuck are just begging the police to beat them. When the police do fuck them up, now, they're happy.)

Some folks will make idle threats to a cop. People that don't give a fuck will back their threats up with action. They will fight the police. The officer at the scene can't talk to them nor treat them civil and shouldn't waste his time trying. Go right into police mode and police them. Lock them up if you have to. Fuck them up if they make you. By any means necessary. Look at the situation, determine how many officers he'll need to handle it and when the help arrives, it's time to get busy. Here's the proof.

Example: The fool at the E2 nightclub

One night, I was working with my partner Freddie. We were at the E2 nightclub when we were approached by a very, very pretty woman. She ran up to me. She was crying hysterically. I calmed her down and asked her what happened. She said that a man in the club (A man she did not know) came up behind her, reached under her skirt and began to feel on her ass. As she was telling us this, here comes Mr. Man. "That's him there," she said. Freddie and I stepped to him. Here was his explanation for disrespecting the woman: "Yo' dog!! I done spent $300.00 in this motherfucking club tonight." I took out my baton, stepped in his face and said, "Yo' dog. I'm going in the club right now and spend $400.00. When I come out, I get to fuck you in your fat ass, alright?" No? Click. Click. Handcuffs. The lady signed complaints and that fool went where fools belong. The moral of the story? These people don't have respect for anyone, including themselves. They sure as hell ain't gonna give a police officer any respect so the officer must take it by force. That's how the police turn people that don't give a fuck into people that give a fuck now.

5. People with a death wish

These are the very few and the very dangerous. Large caliber weapons were designed with these folks in mind. They've got their minds made up and are prepared to die. The police will not take them in alive. They are holding court on the streets and they will kill you. The time and energy an officer spends lifting weights, running around a track, hitting the heavy bag and shooting at the gun range is for this elite group. The hell with arresting them. You kill them on sight. This is not the time to be thinking about rules, regulations, public opinion or civil litigation. You get a shot. You take it. Shoot to kill.

I never met one face to face in my career. I did see two on television. Back in 1997, two bank robbers with fully automatic assault rifles, body armor from head to toe and a few semi auto pistols took on the entire LAPD. Those robbers were not going to surrender and were prepared to kill anyone that got in the way. Talking to them would be a waste of time. What would you say? "Stop in the name of the law!" "Drop your weapon!" At the rate of fire they were shooting, a policeman would be dead before he got that shit out of his mouth. The moral of the story? Herb Bailey, my mentor, had a saying about these kinds of people. HB would say, "T-Man. That motherfucker must be tired of having birthday parties."

CHAPTER 4

Don't Say It And Don't Ask

A police officer is trained to be polite to the citizens he serves and to keep a professional demeanor. It is easy to be professional when an officer is dealing with someone civilized. Not so easy when he is dealing with a screaming, cursing, ignorant asshole. The freedom of speech is a constitutional right. The public has every right to question the law. An officer tries to leave a citizen with a good taste in his mouth when the interaction is over. So by all means, ask questions if you have any. However, you don't have to get nasty. If you do, street laws require that the police officer get nasty with you.

Street laws are the rules that apply in the concrete jungle. Even amongst the lawless in society, there are laws. Violate the laws of the streets and your ass will get dealt with. As agents of the criminal laws, an officer must also be well versed in the laws of the streets. On the streets, the greatest violation is disrespect. Disrespect will be dealt with immediately, directly, and with extreme prejudice. If a citizen does not show a police officer any respect, the police officer won't show the citizen any. This is not professional conduct and it violates department policy. That's just the way it is on the streets.

What's the first street law that children are taught? If somebody hits you, you hit them back. A cop's reputation is on the line. The word spreads fast on the streets. A police officer who lets himself get "punked" on the streets, in the public eye, is fucked. That officer will get no respect. Now, if that officer fucks somebody up in the public eye, that word spreads fast too.

The highest ranking police officials across the nation know that this is true. When they were working the streets, alleys and projects, they did the same thing. Very few will admit to it in public because: 1. They don't want to lose the position that they've risen to. 2. They are in a position now where they don't have to deal with the bullshit anymore.

Police officers do not make the rules. They just enforce the rules. The public should take their complaints to the politicians that make the rules and have the power to change the rules. Instead, they take their frustrations out on the policeman. It's not what you say as much as how you say it and for every action, there's going to be a reaction.

(On a personal note: Over the course of my career, I put up with the complaints, gripes, bitching and moaning from the public. I was paid to take verbal abuse. I wasn't paid to kiss nobody's ass! If a citizen said some ignorant shit to me, street laws were applied. What follows are some of the most popular snide remarks, statements and questions that were thrown at me during the "heat of the moment" by John Q Public. Always remember that you, the citizen, started it. The answer or the comeback will be served to you the same way you served it to me. Hot, mild, or spicy.)

You asked the question. I gave you the answer

Q. "Do I look like a criminal?" A. "Yes"

Q. "All these people out here shooting each other and you're arresting me?"

A. "I don't see anybody shooting anybody right now. I don't hear any shots being fired right now. You tell me where they're shooting right now. I'll let you go right now. But, you've got to tell me where they're shooting right now. Not 30 minutes from now. Right now."

Q. "Why ain't you catching some real criminals?"

A. "I am. Didn't I just catch you?"

Q. "Officer, don't you see them fighting over there?"

A. "They're fighting over there? Well, they ain't fighting over here. That's a job for the "over there" police officer. I'm over here."

Q. "Can you give me a break?"

A. "Not today."

Q. "You're trying to make sergeant?"

A. "Not today."

Q. "Where were you at when my house got burglarized?"

A. "I was at my house with a cold beer in my left hand and a 9mm. in my right hand. I knew somebody's house was gonna get broken into that night. It wasn't gonna be mine."

Q. "Why did the police shoot him so many times?"
A. "The same reason the fire department used all that water. Is the fire out?"

Q. "Why didn't the cops just shoot the gun/knife/baseball bat out his hands?"
A. "Police officers are just like civilians. They don't want to get shot, stabbed or beat with bats. They'd do the same thing you'd do if you were attacked with a deadly weapon and you had a gun in your hand." (Note: In his autobiography, Larry Bird (a shooter) said only two words entered his mind when shooting free throws. All net. Policemen apply the same logic when shooting people. Only the words are different. Police officers think: Center mass. Head shot.) "Shoot the gun out his hand? That would make you either a damn good shot or a damn fool."

Q. "Why you got your gun out, officer?"
A. "Because it's mine, sir."

Here's the scene. A gang fight. 10 people fighting. 20 people watching. Two policemen arrive. Trust me. One of those 20 people watching is gonna ask:

Q. "Oh!! Y'all gonna just let them fight?"
A. (Hand him your baton.) "You go stop them with this stick Bruce Lee."

Q. "Officer. If you're in this restaurant eating, who's on the streets protecting me?"

A. "Nobody. So pull up a chair and get something to eat."

Q. "What!! You working for the white man now?"

A. "You damn right. When I get a $20 bill, I'm looking for Andrew Jackson, not Samuel L Jackson. George Washington, not Denzel Washington. Benjamin Franklin, not Aretha Franklin."

Q. "You stopped me cause I'm black?"

A. "Yes. Plus, you're 5'10", 170 lbs, dark skinned, with braids, wearing a white T-shirt, baggy, low-riding blue jeans and Air Force Ones. Tomorrow, wear a three piece suit and see how many times the police stop you."

You made the statement. Now, prepare for the comeback

S. "I bet the police don't do this shit where the white people live."

C. "I wouldn't know. I don't live around white people."

S. "If I had your job officer, I would shoot everybody."

C. "No you wouldn't. You couldn't. And, you shouldn't."

S. "Don't shoot me. I'm reaching for my wallet."

C. "Reach for whatever you want. Your wallet or your gun. If your gun looks like a wallet, you'd better shoot me. Let your wallet look like a gun and see what happens to you."

S. "Y'all needs to be over there where they be selling them drugs."

C. "They be selling them drugs over there? Well, they don't be selling them drugs over here. Right now, I be over here. That sounds like something to do when I be over there."

The scene: I'm making an arrest. Once I handcuff my prisoner, he goes off.

S. "Hit me motherfucker!! Hit me motherfucker!!" (Note: You will never see a prisoner get in a police dog's face and yell, "Bite me motherfucker!!")

C. "I'm not going to hit you, sir. You want to file a lawsuit and get rich. I need you to stay poor and ignorant so I can arrest you again."

S. "I ain't Rodney King."

C. "I noticed that. Did you notice that we're not in Los Angeles. Rodney got his ass whipped in LA. You're gonna get your ass whipped in Chicago."

S. "Take these cuffs off me officer and I'll beat your motherfucking ass."

C. "Excuse me? The time to beat my ass was when I walked up to you and your hands were free. I told you to turn around and you did. I told you to put your hands behind your back and you did. Then, I put these cuffs on you. That was me who put these cuffs on you."

S. "You ain't shit without that gun and that badge."

C. "Never you mind about this gun and badge. It's this baton you need to be worried about. That's what I'll be beating your ass with."

S. "I hope you get shot!!" (The last act of a desperate man who ran out of insults. That's a cold thing to say. The policeman must comeback colder.)

C. "Do you own a gun or can you borrow one for a day? Yeah? Great. Why don't you go get the motherfucker and come back and see me. If you want something done right, you should do it yourself. I'll be waiting for you. You punk ass bitch!!" (Now, if he don't go get a gun and come back and see me, what is he? A punk ass bitch.)

Attitude and showmanship are essential tools in a police officer's bag of tricks. These questions and statements are punches being thrown at the police officer. A good cop must be a good counter puncher. Like I said citizen. You did start it.

CHAPTER 5

THE TRAFFIC TICKET

Drivers do not like getting traffic tickets. The police know this. Why do police officers write traffic tickets? They have to do it. It's part of their job. Imagine, for a minute, you play for the Chicago Bulls. Now, let's say after 25 games, you haven't scored a point, blocked a shot, grabbed a rebound, stole a pass, missed every free throw shot you took and you don't have an assist. After 25 games!! How long do you think you'll keep your job? If a policeman doesn't score any points, what good is he to the team?

Most people that have a close encounter with a cop will have it while driving their car. The best way to avoid a traffic ticket is simple. Follow the rules of the road. Most traffic violations are minor infractions, punishable by fines only. Drivers feel that when they commit a traffic violation, the police officer should dismiss it. It ain't no big thing.

Everything is relative. Armed robbery is a little thing when you compare it to first degree murder. However, if you suddenly found yourself on a dark street, looking down the barrel of a .357 magnum, armed robbery will become a big thing to you.

Law enforcement is the only job I ever had where the customer didn't want me to do my job. Take a look at Michael Jordan. At work, Michael didn't have one job. He had two. Job #1. Win the ball game. Job #2. Put on a show. That's what the customer wanted to see and he paid good money to see it. When MJ stole the basketball and started racing down an open court, did the customer want him to pass the ball up court to John Paxson. Hell no.

The customer didn't pay all that money to see a lay up. He paid to see a dunk by Air Jordan. At the least, pass it to Scottie Pippin. The customer could live with that. Scottie was a slam dunk machine too.

A rookie will write a traffic ticket faster than a veteran will (remember that hard-on he's got). Officers assigned to traffic units have to write tickets. That's their bread and butter. Writing tickets is not "taking a bite out of crime." Ticket writing raises revenue for the city. (Note: On the other hand, I've seen many people lose their lives in car crashes. Too many.)

A driver can talk himself out of a ticket or he can talk himself into multiple tickets. The best thing to do during a traffic stop is to listen, don't talk. The policeman pulled you over so he wants to talk to you. Pass the "attitude test" and you might not get a ticket. You might get a lecture instead. If the driver knows what he did, admit it. If he doesn't know what he did, say he doesn't know. It would be in the best interest of the driver not to ask the police officer to give him a break right off the top. (Why should the officer give him a break?)

Here are the steps he should take at a traffic stop: 1. Listen to what the officer has to say. 2. Acknowledge that he made a mistake or state that he doesn't know what he did wrong. 3. Try to give a plausible reason why he did what he did. 4. Hope he passes the "attitude test." 5. Hope that he is dealing with an officer that gives the test.

Now, the worst thing a driver can do at a traffic stop is to argue with the police officer at the scene. Look around you. You are not in traffic court. That's where you argue your case. What usually ends any further discussion during a traffic dispute? When the driver tells the policeman, "Yes I did" or "No I didn't." To the police officer, that's translated to mean, "Officer, you're a god damn liar!" Now, it's ticket time.

Warning!!!!! There is one police officer I should tell you about. You may have met him. Most drivers know him as Officer Asshole. This cop doesn't give breaks to anyone. His real name is Officer N.E.A.T. (No Excuses Accepted Today). If you haven't met him yet, one day you will. Should you run into him, just take the ticket. There is nothing that you can say or do to get a break. Nothing. Officer N.E.A.T. doesn't care who you are, who your husband or wife is, if you have family on the police force, that you're just running a little late for work, etc. Officer N.E.A.T. is an asshole, has always been an asshole and loves being an asshole.

There is one instance when the public does want the policeman to do his job and write traffic tickets. It's when they become the victim of someone's negligent driving. You stopped at your stop sign going westbound. But, the car going northbound doesn't stop at their stop sign. Crash!! Now, that driver going westbound (that's you) wants the policeman to pull out the rules of the road play book ("Check his driver's license, insurance, search his car, look in his eyes, smell his breath, make him walk a straight line"). Now, it seems that traffic enforcement is a big thing after all.

There are some drivers that feel they should never receive a ticket. White people believe that they're too white to get a ticket. Female drivers will resort to tears to get out of a ticket. Sometimes it works and sometimes it doesn't.

Real pretty women think that they're too pretty to get a ticket. I have news for all the pretty women of the world. It's not called a "court date" for nothing. I will see your pretty ass again. In about 30 days.

CHAPTER 6

THE DEPARTMENT

"A boss is like a diaper. Always on your ass and usually full of shit." Whoever came up with that analogy probably worked for a police department. The superintendents, commissioners, deputy chiefs, majors and other department heads of police departments across America forget something as they rise through the ranks. The higher up they go, the least important they become. It doesn't matter how many stars, bars, oak leaves or scrambled egg clusters they wear on their uniforms. The value that they bring to their department can not be measured in their pay scale. The most important division in any major police department is the patrol division. The foot soldiers do the work. The department brass take the credit for the job well done.

If three supervisors are scheduled to work and only one shows up, there's no need to panic. If thirty patrolmen are on the sheets and only ten show up, it's panic time. Who's gonna man the cars?

A good supervisor will let his officers do their job without interference (unless they're messing up). Officers really don't want a supervisor standing there looking over their shoulder unless they need one there. They don't mind the good supervisors on the scene. It's the bad ones that police officers hate to see coming. Some cause more trouble than they prevent. (I called them "fight promoters." Don King with stars, bars and white shirts.) Sgt. He/ She would arrive on the scene, get tempers flared up and then give the order: "Lock him up!" Then, that supervisor would watch from ringside (just like Don King does) as the patrolmen fight the fight he/she started.

The pledge of allegiance that a police officer has toward management only goes as high as a commanding officer is considered a "friend." There is very little allegiance toward a "boss." Just listen to them talk. A "boss" will tell on himself and so will a "friend." How does a commanding officer lose the allegiance of his troops? It's easy. If he does any of the following, he won't have any of his men or women on his side.

1. DON'T GIVE HIS TROOPS THE CREDIT THAT THEY DESERVE. He won't give them credit for showing up to work on time, in uniform, hitting the streets and working their beats. It's easy to tell his troops to do something that he didn't do himself. Policemen with time on the job see co-workers get promoted and are well aware of the work ethic of the newly promoted officers. A veteran can take orders from a supervisor that proved himself while in the rank and file. If he didn't put in work as a trooper, he can forget it. Rank will be respected. That doesn't mean the supervisor will be respected.
2. MAKE HIS TROOPS FEEL THAT THEY ARE EXPENDABLE AND THEIR JOBS ARE AT RISK. When a commanding officer comes in the roll call room and all he can talk about is suspensions, reassignments, disciplining officers and terminations, that boss just fucked up big time. Never mind the fact that on any given day, a police officer can get his brains

blown out. There's enough stress just working the streets. Now, he's got a boss threatening his livelihood. There are times that management should come down on the troops. The whole concept of a police force is that they work together. That's what makes the police force a "force." Address those officers that weaken the force. Do not threaten the "working police" or you'll be sorry you did.

3. TREAT HIS TROOPS LIKE A BEAST OF BURDEN. Their only function in life is to work, work and work. Write more tickets. Make more arrest. Give me more, more, more. (Note: I can't pull a criminal out of my ass. If it's not there, it's not there.) To a boss, it's all about numbers. Why? Because, the numbers can make the boss look good or make him look bad. That's all a boss cares about. He doesn't give a damn about his troops. He has a slave master's mentality. ("Fill up that cotton sack, boy!!") This is not the way to get a veteran officer's attention. The boss doesn't know it, but he just turned a working police officer into one who will do just enough work to shut him up. A "friend" will get a couple of tickets a day from that police officer. However, since the boss came to the officer with that "Master Charlie" bullshit; that sucker will be lucky if he gets 2 tickets a week. The boss can't whip the officer. Write two tickets a week and the boss can't fire him either. You know why? The officer has to go to traffic court.

Every police chief, captain, lieutenant and sergeant that a police officer works under will promise to "back him up if he's in the right." Truth be told, in most cases, he doesn't need them to back him up if he's right. The evidence will be all the back up he needs. What about the gray areas? The judgment calls? That's when a cop needs the department to back him up.

It one thing to be the boss and another thing to be too bossy. When the supervisor is doing his job and the patrolman's job too, he becomes a P.I.T.A. Pain in the ass. The three most important letters in law enforcement are C, Y, and A (Cover your ass). Failure to CYA has lead to many officers losing their jobs. When you take it to the extreme, CYA stands for the coward you are. I had one sergeant who tried to justify everything he did by saying he's just covering his ass.

The Chicago Police Department, like most major police departments, has a list of Department General Orders. In Chicago, they are approved by the Superintendent of Police, the highest ranking police officer within the department. You would think that if something was done per the general orders, that should be good enough. It's good enough for the superintendent. Not good enough for my sergeant. He had his own set of orders.

Per the general orders, a burglary did not require an immediate notification to a detective unit unless: 1. The loss was greater than $20,000.00. 2. Efforts were made to defeat/circumvent an alarm system. 3. The break-in or attempted break-in of a safe. (Note: If it was newsworthy, say like, President Obama's house got hit, you might wanna give the dicks a courtesy call.)

My sergeant would have a patrolman calling the detectives to notify them of the burglary of a case of soda pop, a box of donuts and a bag of potato chips. In Chi-Town, this will not lead to a C.S.I. investigation.

The patrolman on the phone is wasting the detective's time and, quite frankly, pissing him off. The detective is on the phone thinking, "Who is this fool calling me at three in the morning to tell me about the theft of some kid's lunch snacks?"

When they work for a "friend," the troops will work. I remember one friend in particular. He worked with my mentor Herb in the narcotics division for many years. Herb told me, "T-Man, Pete is a warrior. He's the real police." He came to my district as a field lieutenant. When I first saw him, I knew he was the real thing. After a few roll calls, I could tell just by the way he talked to the troops that he was not a "boss." He told on himself.

Whenever the lieutenant gave roll call, he'd tell you your assignment for the night. If you had court, he'd let you know. What made the lieutenant different was what he talked about after all the shop talk. He never talked about writing tickets, catching curfews or making arrests. That wasn't important to the lieutenant. He talked about officer safety. Each time. Every time. Check those corners. Watch their hands. Back each other up. Go home safe to your family. When his officers went out on patrol, they knew that they were working for someone who cared more about them than about how many tickets they wrote a night.

All police officers graduate from the same academy. You can't really equate rank with intelligence. One might not have anything to do with the other. A baboon can write a traffic ticket if you teach him. It doesn't take a genius to be a cop. A police officer with years of experience would be a damn fool to follow any advise from a supervisor solely on rank alone. When you let someone else think for you, you put your life in someone else's hands.

On a Personal Note

When the public fears for their life or the loss of their property, they pick up a phone and call the police to come to their rescue. Who do the police have to come to their rescue? With only a few exceptions, the police officer has no one. The police are against everybody. Criminals are against the police for obvious reasons. The feeling is mutual, so that's not a problem. The community is against the police. They don't want the police around until they need them. Police officers accept this fact, so that's not a problem. The media is against the police. Good news about the police does not sell like bad news. The police understand that, so that's not a problem. Community activist are against the police because the community is. If the activist sided with the police, they would become police activist and out of a job. Police officers accept them for what they are, so that's not a problem. In 2007, the Mayor of Chicago turned against the police. Now, the police had a problem.

The mayor delivered a hard slap to the face of the Chicago PD that year. He was appointing a new Superintendent of Police and had dozens of qualified candidates within the department to choose from. Who did he select? He choose a man from outer space. The mayor showed every member of the CPD what he thought of them with that move. To hell with all of you! The new superintendent was fighting an uphill battle for acceptance. He had never worn a CPD uniform before he was hired. How can a rookie tell veteran police officers how to police a city and the rookie just landed on the planet?

Throughout my years on the police force, the perception was this: nepotism reigns supreme. The "good old boys" system. Those in command were just waiting for retirement to pass the baton to their heirs. It was unwritten in stone that if you were not a member or friend to the royal family, you would not reach the upper echelon of the department. The general consensus amongst the troops was the new superintendent was brought in to buck the system. Being an outsider, he wouldn't feel beholden to anyone under his command except the man that hired him. He would have free reign to run the CPD as he saw fit. No more favors, phone calls or clout.

The department had been getting some bad ink in the press around this time. (A footnote: The mayor had also been called downtown to a closed door meeting at the federal building around this time too. Hmm.) The mayor was under pressure to make changes. Now, he had to choose who to make happy. The last people the mayor thought about making happy were his police officers. Making these changes would require the mayor to hurt some feelings. He didn't want to look familiar faces in the eye as he stabbed them in the back. He let the new chief be the bearer of the bad news coming.

The new Superintendent of Police came in the door chopping heads off. He gave the department heads an ultimatum. Get demoted, get reassigned or get out. The media played it up big in bold print. There's a new sheriff in town! The superintendent should have thanked the media as much as he thanked the mayor for the job. Between the news coverage of an off duty CPD police officer beating up a little white lady in a bar, another bar fight involving off duty CPD officers and a group of dumb ass policemen, working in an elite unit of the CPD who were caught stealing money from drug dealers, the media did what they do best. Make a mountain out of a mosquito bite.

I had worked for five superintendents prior to the new chief in 2007. Who ran the CPD was of no concern to me. My concerns did not reach that high up the chain of command. I only had three concerns as a patrolman. 1. Who is my watch commander? 2. Who is my sergeant? 3. Who is my partner? In my 24 years of service, I was never, ever on the streets, handling my business, looked over to my left or my right and saw the Superintendent of the Chicago Police Department handling the business with me. I didn't expect to see the new chief either.

Fair or unfair, the new chief in 2007 was not welcomed with open arms. He used to work for the FBI. Translated, that means he was a lawman. He just wasn't The Police. The troops could not relate to him and didn't think that he could relate to them. On top of all that, add the fact that he didn't pay his dues on the city streets and now, the troops didn't respect him. When he spoke about the City of Chicago and the CPD, the message would have little impact with the rank and file because he was an alien. In order to truly love an organization, you've got to invest time and energy in it. Money can't buy you love. A hefty salary does not mean that you love an organization. Maybe in time, he will feel the love for the Chicago Police Department.

CHAPTER 7

THE MEDIA

When does a police story become front page news? When the police screw up, get locked up, or when an officer is killed in the line of duty. A major drug seizure or a high profile arrest may make the front page. Positive press about the police usually gets a mention in the local news section. When the story cast a negative reflection on the police department, it's on the front page, in bold print, and the pictures are in color. Crack cocaine, gangs and guns made being a cop in the 80's, 90's and 2000's a very dangerous occupation. They weren't all the dangers an officer had to face. The media (through news reports, the cinema, rap music, etc.) helped add to the dangers an officer had to face.

An old drinking buddy of mine told me once: "Free whiskey will kill you."

Free money will too. Remember the old public aid system? A good idea that turned bad. It was supposed to be just that. Aid. Assistance until you got on your feet. When you did, you moved on up and moved on out of the system. What did it become ultimately? A way of life. Did the aid system give people that needed a job a job? No. It gave them free money. It gave more women more money for having more babies. Provided them with an overcrowded, poverty ridden, crime infested neighborhood to live in. It gave healthy, able bodied men general assistance checks instead of steady work. Add to this mix a hefty dose of gangs, guns, and the most addictive and affordable drug ever. Add it all up and what do you get? Murder. Madness. Mayhem. News.

Crack spread like cancer in poor neighborhoods and government dollars provided a large percentage of the money drug dealers made. Dealers went from making hundreds selling marijuana to making millions selling the rock. While the money flowed in, so did the violence. Earned money builds your self esteem. Free money stunts your growth and kills any desire to improve yourself. Generation after generation of lost potential. Thousands of people "waiting for my check." Some learn to accept this as their fate. Only a few break free from the cycle.

The media harps on the negative side of life. "If it bleeds, it leads." Making a living off the pain and suffering of others. The media loves to hate the police. The media and the police do share one thing in common. They both stick their nose into other people's business. In the case of the police, the people usually call 911. The media will comes to your house unannounced and uninvited, walk up to you, stick a microphone in your face and start asking a whole lot of questions that are none of their business. Journalist write newspaper articles on people who did not ask to be the topic of their article. Photographers and cameramen will take your picture without asking for your permission. If the media feels that they have a constitutional right to walk up to someone who's minding his own business and start asking him personal questions, taking his picture and invading his space; that person should have a constitutional right to knock their ass out.

The "cop movie" has always been popular in Hollywood. Dirty Harry. Lethal Weapon. Die Hard. Training Day. These movies are entertaining, not realistic. One movie that looked into the mind of the street cop was Dark Blue starring Kurt Russell. A movie about a good cop who did a bad thing. He did it for the right reason, but he was wrong for doing it. Why did he do it? He let someone else think for him. (Note: A "high five" to HBO's "The Wire." The best police series ever created to date. That show was too real.)

The best police movie I ever saw wasn't a police movie. It was an army movie. Platoon. The police department is the army for a city. The first line of defense. Every time I watch Platoon, I see every kind of police officer I ever worked with and every kind of supervisor I ever worked under.

Tom Berenger (Barnes) and Willem Dafoe (Elias) were The Real Police. Elias was a warrior with a lot of heart. His heart got in the way. In battle, you have to pick a side and stay there. Charlie Sheen (Chris) was a rookie who became The Police by the end of the movie. In a fight, you get three options. Win, lose, or draw. But, only if you fight back. Reggie Johnson (Junior) was A Police Officer. Went to sleep on guard duty and could have gotten everyone in the platoon killed. He was worthless and deserved to die slow. Barnes was not the enemy. He had just been in the army too long. That's why he snapped. In a war, you need true warriors to win. To survive in battle, you do what you must do. People die in battle. Some are innocent. Some are guilty. Don't act and it might be you. Barnes was a leader and every team needs a leader.

(Note: I saw myself in Keith David (King). King knew exactly how important he was in the big picture. He didn't count for shit and he accepted it. He was just a name on a dog tag. I was just a number on a badge. King had the perfect attitude for a cop: "Just keep your dick hard and your powder dry and you will get out of here. Don't be no fool and don't think too much. Ain't no such thing as a coward out here.")

Gangster rap. That music is responsible for more inner city youth being beat up by the police than anything else. These rappers tell kids to say, "Fuck the police!" The kids admire them, so they listen. The rap star is not going to post the kid's bail, pay his legal fees, visit the kid in the county jail or in the hospital. Rappers like to brag about getting shot and surviving. (Note: They got shot because they didn't run fast enough. You got shot, fool!! What the hell do you have to brag about?) The 1980's produced the largest crop of "I don't give a fuck" people in the history of thug life. The 1990's produced even more.

In the studio, rappers always win the fight. They brainwash these kids. Young people see the clothes, the cars, the money, the "bling bling" and they want it too. The lifestyle is not the issue I have with rappers. It's the message they convey to youngsters as to how they achieved the lifestyle that I have an issue with. Damn going to school. Get your degree from sidewalk academy. Buy you some "merch." Cook it, cut it and sell it. Get rich or die trying. You got "beef" with a nigger, you smoke the motherfucker! The rappers say it and the kids buy into it.

There are too, too many young boys and girls who identify how down they are by how tough they are. They try to prove their toughness through acts of violence. Drive-by shooters ain't tough. Suicide bombers are.

Like a lot of policemen, I worked part time jobs when I was off the clock at the PD. The job I had the longest was security for the Chicago Public Schools. I worked at Parkside Academy for 10 years. On most days, I knew I was working in an elementary school with young boys and girls. There were a few days that I thought I was working in the Cook County Jail. I worked there for two reasons (I did get paid so make it three). Reason 1. The staff and the students. The children grew on me as time went by. They expected to see me there every day. I was their officer and they were my kids. For every one I wanted to choke, there were ten I wanted to help. The teachers were devoted to their students and I felt like a part of the team.

Reason 2. The annual day of child abuse. Every year, without fail, the Parkside Panthers boy's basketball team would challenge us (the staff) to a basketball game. Every year, without fail, we (the staff) would teach those boys a valuable lesson. You don't send a boy to do a man's job. The ass whipping we would put on those boys was just short of aggravated child abuse. We would win by 15, 20, 30 points. One year, we won by 43 points. That was with the dream team of Mr. Wilborn, Coach O'Neal, Mr. Bartel, myself, and the MVP, Mr. Wiafe. We beat them like they owed us money. We also got their attention and their respect. In the end, we got their love.

I had many, many long talks with the children about the gangster mentality some of them had. When I'm dealing with teenagers, I tend to be a little understanding. They're young, dumb, and lack the maturity to think like adults. I used to tell them that if they persist in their way of thinking, they're gonna look pretty in their coffin. They'll be dead before they turn 20 years old. Their face will be on a R.I.P. T-shirt.

(On a personal note: I used to think I had a tough job until I started working at Parkside. Teachers in public school systems have a tough, thankless job. They come to work to teach their students and some students come only because their mother said, "Get your ass out the bed and go to school!!" They deal with children from the worst environments. Broken homes where they're neglected, abused and sometimes abandoned, both physically and emotionally. Now, that teacher has to try to teach him/her.

Three or four bad apples will spoil the the whole classroom. What's most disappointing is that when things go bad with the child, the parents always want to blame the teachers. The teachers are there every day. The parents only comes to school on report card pick-up day and now they want to complain. God bless teachers.)

How does a police officer become a hero? A surefire, no-doubt-about-it hero? Get killed in the line of duty. The more violently he dies, the more certain he'll be regarded as a hero. Now, he wasn't a hero just for coming to work and he might not be one if he goes home in one piece. Take a fatal gunshot. Instant hero. When the World Trade buildings fell on those police and firemen on 9/11, they became heroes. That's what had to happen before those men and women were appreciated.

People will become bitter when they don't feel appreciated. Police officers are no different. They go to work with the best of intentions.

Try to do their job and when they do, they expect a "thank you." What do the police get? Disrespected, spit at, shot at, bricks and bottles thrown at them, bags of feces thrown at them. The greatest fear an officer will experience is being shot at. In most cases, he doesn't even know where the shots are coming from. He just ducks. Now, imagine this scenario. You're a cop. You see a man on the street with a gun and as you approach him, he starts shooting at you. He turns and runs away but you chase him down into a dead end alley. Now, he throws his gun to the ground and says, "I give up. Don't shoot." What should you do? The laws of the courts say you should take him before a judge. The laws of the streets say you should kill his ass right there in that alley! You'd better take him in because if you kill him, the rhyming reverends might object.

The rhyming reverends are like toilet paper. Just hanging around waiting for some shit to go down. They walk into the lion's den when the lion ain't in. Take hundreds of people and news cameras with them too. It's safe to walk into a war zone after they tell NBC, ABC, CBS, CNN and Fox news when they're going.

I have written a poem for the reverends: "When the shit is going down, the rhyming reverends can't be found. The very next day, they've got plenty to say. They march en masse when the police kick ass. Talk big shit from a church pulpit. They need to stay in their place and pray for peace. They're just rhyming reverends. They ain't the police."

They fire the crowd up with their speeches. However, when those television lights turn off and the news reporters start packing up to leave, the reverends are leaving right with them and they're not coming back. They are going back to their homes and leaving behind that crowd of people that they just told that they're there for them. The crowd has nowhere to go. They live in the neighborhood. When the problems return (drug dealing, gang recruiting, drive-by shootings, etc.), who are they gonna call?

The reverends don't mean any harm and they do want to help the people. They also want the photo-op. I used to get angry whenever I saw them rhyming on television. Then, it hit me. They aren't any different than the millions of men who sit their fat, sloppy, out of shape asses in front of the television on game day and say: "He should has caught that pass." "He should have made that shot." "He should have hit that pitch." "He should have made that tackle." These men sit in their recliner chairs, drinking beer, passing gas and eating pizza, talking like it's easy to be a world class athlete. If it was that easy, they would be out there earning those millions.

There will never be a riot over the murder of a police officer. Those high profile activist who march for any alleged human injustice do not march for murdered policemen. (Let the police shot someone and it's on.) The murder of a police officer is acceptable. It doesn't cause an uproar. There might be a moment of silence as you read about the deceased officer's bio: 29 years old, a five year veteran of the force, married with a child and another one on the way. There may be some sorrow felt. But, it will pass as soon as you find out that the lawn mower you wanted to buy is on sale at Home Depot. 20% off.

What the rhyming reverends need to happen to them is an up close and personal dose of the real thing. Not the next day when the crime scene has been processed and the police tape is pulled down. They need to see it in real time when the tempers are flaring and the bullets and bricks are flying.

Until they do, they don't have a clue.

How did the media add to the danger an officer faced on the streets? Two words. Rodney King. That really changed the game. Thanks to the media, that video was ingrained into the minds of every citizen in the country. It sent a shock wave that was felt by every police department in America. Even though it happened in Los Angeles, I heard people in Chicago saying, "Look at how the police do you." (Notice they said "the police." Not the LAPD.) The media coverage was overkill. 5 o'clock news. 6 o'clock news. 10 o'clock news. For days. Weeks. The media drove it in the ground.

In Chapter 3, I spoke about the Five People police officers encounter on the streets. Rodney King is a classic example of Group #4. He could have pulled his car over when the first police car got behind him with lights and sirens. He choose to keep driving. When any driver gets behind the wheel of a car, there are certain rules that the driver must abide by. He gives his implied consent to follow these rules for the privilege of driving a car. He knows what they are. Driver's license. Insurance. Drive a safe vehicle. Don't drink and drive, etc. And, he will curb his vehicle when instructed to do so by a police vehicle that has activated it's emergency equipment. He doesn't have an option to pull over only when he feels like it.

As a former police officer, I can say that those officers on that video did nothing wrong in getting him on the ground. He choose to fight the law and the law won. The officers did what they were trained to do with an uncooperative subject. The baton strikes, the taser use, even the kicks were textbook use of force. The public wants to act like a number 4. They want the police to treat them like a number 1. That's not how it goes in the real world.

As a former police officer, I can also say that even though they used the right tactics, the problem was in how "much" tactics they used. Once he went down, they should have backed off. Now, if he gets back up? "Down goes Frazier!" It is safer for the policemen involved not to get in a wrestling match. Police officers carry guns. Wrestling with a man on the ground is a good way to lose control of their weapons, be killed with their own gun and their partner too, It's tactically safer to never let a subject put his hands on them. That's what batons are for. That's what taser guns are for. Pain compliance. That way, policemen don't have to use deadly force.

When the Rodney King video became worldwide news, I began to notice that, more and more, the public wanted to fight the police. Fighting the police became the new lottery. If you got the right number (of kicks, punches and baton strikes), you could get paid. The civil lawsuit became a matter of great concern to the city fathers. Police chiefs and mayors are now scared to death.

The cost to settle these civil suits was rising into the millions. The police departments must be re-invented. More sensitivity training.

Taser guns. Pepper spray. The police departments must use less force. The police officers on the street must kiss more ass.

This school of thought was gonna be a hard sell to officers from the B.R.K. (Before Rodney King) era. It's hard to bend a grown tree. Police brutality was unacceptable in 1986, the year I was hired. The definition of what police brutality was changed after Rodney King. The new definition was that "any" force used against the public that caused them injury was considered excessive force. CPD officers used to carry long, metal flashlights in my rookie days. They could light up a dark room. In a fight, they could light your ass up. When the CPD issued me a 7 inch plastic flashlight and ordered me to get rid of my "Kale" light, I saw the writing on the wall. The department was saying, "Here you go. Now, go out there and arrest them, but don't hurt them. We can't afford it anymore. We can only afford to bury you, officer. We have to choose between officer safety or our money. We choose our money."

The Chicago Fire Department doesn't realize how good they've got it. The mayor, the fire chief, the media and the public wants to see the fire department whip the fire's ass. No one wants to see policemen whip ass. If they do, it's police brutality. Does the mayor, the media or the public ever ask the question, "What did he do?" No. Why? Because it doesn't matter.

On a Personal Note

One moment in time can change history. I was an eyewitness to one. The Rodney King incident. The beginning of the end. That video could be featured on a reality show. "Bullies. Caught on Tape." The police have long been viewed as the bully on the block. No one likes a bully. Especially the people that get bullied by him. Who gets bullied by the police the most? Black and Hispanic men. The lower class. Just imagine the public outrage if Rodney King was White and the cops were Black or Hispanic. The mayor and the police chief in LA would have had a heart attack over that video.

As a child growing up, there were two people that I knew not to talk back to. My father and my mother. Why? Because if I did, they would whip my ass. It was never about me agreeing with what they told me to do or liking what they told me to do. It was only about doing what they told me to do. My parent's orders were not open to discussion. The choice was simple. Do what they said or deal with the consequences. A long time ago, the same rules applied when the public dealt with a police officer.

I thought that once I became an adult, there'd be no one to tell me what to do. Wrong! As long as I live, there's always gonna be someone, at some point in time, telling me what to do.

The public may never have been in love with the policeman, but they didn't blatantly disrespect the police officer a long time ago. Those few who did got to experience the "serve" side of serve and protect. (Translation. The police would kick your ass.) However, just like a parent that will whip his child for being disrespectful; that same parent will kill a motherfucker for messing with his child. The child didn't just receive discipline. The child also received support and protection. In many ways, this is how the policeman views the public he serves.

When I worked the streets, I felt that my job was to protect the weak and the helpless from the bully. I put my life on the line to protect their lives and their property. I got paid to do it, but that's irrelevant. When a citizen called 911, I'm coming. I can get to you in 3 minutes or I can get to you in 8 minutes. When I'm driving through your neighborhood and you shoot at my car, throw bricks and bottles at me, or tell me, "Stop fucking with us" or "Leave us alone," when you call 911 next time, you just pushed my arrival time to 25 minutes and 48 seconds. This is how the public fucks themselves. The police used to try and win the game and get there quick. Now, some officers just play the game. Get there, write a report and move on.

The public can (and will) stand up and defy the police officer nowadays. It feels good to stand up to the bully. Now, the bad news. There are other bullies in the world. The bully without a job. He doesn't need a job because he has a .357 magnum and will stick that gun in your face and take your money. You won't be talking to him like you talked to that armed police officer because this bully can shoot your ass and if you talk too much shit, he will. The bully that likes flat screen televisions but doesn't have the money to buy one. He doesn't need the money. Why? Last night, he saw you unloading a brand new 50 inch TV from your car and take it into your house. All he has to do now is wait for you to go to work.

You can't go to work and watch your house at the same time so what do you do? You install a home security system. If that alarm goes off, who does the alarm company call to check for a break in? The same beat officer who last week you told to leave you alone. Be careful what you wish for. You just might get it. If you keep telling the police to leave you alone, that's just what they will do. They will leave you alone. All alone.

CHAPTER 8

Does Racism Still Exist In Law Enforcement?

To some degree or another, all people stereotype each other. Nothing strange about it because we are all raised different. Culturally, there are some things that make us different and things we share in common. Take a look at the news and you can tell (sometimes, not all the time) which race of people committed what crime even before you see their picture on the television screen. Just look at the crime committed. If you turn on the news and hear about a mass murder at the workplace, which race comes to mind first as to who did it? Black man? Hispanic man? Or, pissed off White man?

There is racism in law enforcement just as there is in everything else in this country. People of different colors pass by each other every day. They don't spend any time getting to know each other. They'd rather get their information from the television or the newspaper. What story does the media tell about poor people? 1. They are criminal by nature. 2. They sell drugs and shoot each other. 3. Lazy and don't want to work. 4. Poor people will rob you, rape you, and kill you. In reality, poor people are the nicest people you will ever meet. Their love is genuine, it comes from the heart. Rich people love you for what you have, not for who you are. They will kill you over a life insurance policy or an inheritance. Rich people love money.

Police officers are regular, ordinary people who are raised in a certain environment, just like anyone else. That environment is the basis of their outlook on life, just like anyone else. If you (or I) were placed into a strange environment, you (or I) would experience culture shock. In the poorest neighborhoods, there is a lot of violence. People under constant stress just react that way. They don't have the resources that people with money have.

If you stole $500.00 from Bill Gates, he probably wouldn't go out on the streets looking for you. Now, Jimmie Lee Gates will come looking for you and you knew it when you stole his money. Jimmie Lee is not going to call 911 to file a police report. He ain't gonna call Judge Mathis or Judge Judy either. He is going to look for you, find you, and do something awful to you.

In poor neighborhoods, people always complain about the high police presence on their block. Where do they think the police are gonna be when every 60 minutes someone on the block is shooting a gun, there's an open "dope spot" on both corners serving 24 hours a day, and every three days there's a shooting on the block? Wherever there are more guns, more gangs, more drugs and more 911 calls, there will be more police.

A police officer who "don't take no shit" will be viewed as a racist if he's a different race than the community he's serving and protecting. Policemen see color. They also see character. Some of the "characters" a cop encounters will turn Officer "Friendly" into Officer "I will kick your ass." After the riots in LA over the King verdict, law enforcement officials tried to upgrade the images of their police departments. They began to raise the bar as to who was qualified to wear a gun and a badge.

When I joined the force in 1986, an applicant only needed a G.E.D, be drug free, pass a psych evaluation and have a relatively clean criminal history. Cops used to come from the streets. Now, they come from universities and colleges. The new wave of officers had good educations, but their street IQ was low because some of them weren't from the streets. Some had never been exposed to the harshness that was waiting for them when they hit the streets.

Do police officers target certain people? Of course they do. The cops on the street are answering the 911 calls, taking the reports and making the arrests. Over time, criminals do fit a certain profile and policemen will use their past experience when dealing with them. That's how they survive. Black and Hispanic men are the poster boys of American crime. The newspapers, televisions and movie screens have ingrained that image into the minds of the public. Police case reports and arrest reports have ingrained that fact into the minds of police officers.

Those who complain about racial profiling the loudest are black men. As a black man myself, I can relate to their anger. As a black police officer, I say to my brothers, stop complaining. We brought it on ourselves. All black men have to suffer because of the actions of a few. Black men should be the last ones to complain about racial profiling.

Just like in the NBA. Black men lead the league in all major (crime) statistics.

(On a very personal note: I am not a college graduate. I do not possess a Ph. D. I possess a high school diploma. I don't have a degree in psychology, psychiatry, sociology or any other study of the human mind. I was The Police and not a civil rights activist. I don't have graphs, projection sheets, university studies or data files to illustrate why I say what I say about the black man. I did have 24 years of asking these questions that I already knew the answer to most of the time. I just asked to make it official for the police report. "Who snatched your purse?" "A black man." Who robbed you?" "A black man." "Who stabbed you?" "A black man." "Who shot you?" "A black man." "Who sold you that bag of dope?" "That nigger right there." Now, when you hear this over, and over, and over. Year, after year, after year. Decade after decade, you will tend to profile a particular group of people too. That is not a racist ideology. That's just plain common sense. The City of Chicago did not hire me to try to determine the roots of criminal behavior. The City of Chicago hired me to deal with the criminal behavior and the criminal. My gun was for hire. I was a mercenary, not a missionary.)

The Chicago Police Department has had issues with low officer morale due to race for as long as I was a member. Nepotism is prevalent. Many officers feel that they've been screwed by the CPD and passed over for promotions and assignments. Going back (way back) in the history of the CPD, the department was manned by officers who's last names were prefixed with an "O" or suffixed with a "ski." Nowadays, there is a rainbow of last names. Everybody has a shot. There is one thing that will never change. It's not what you know. It's who you know. That's not racism. That's life.

There is a surefire cure to racism for every police officer on the streets. The losing battle. All policemen should have one in their career (the sooner, the better). Once they get in a losing battle, they will learn to appreciate the help that they get from their fellow officers and be more willing to offer assistance themselves. When a police officer is on the ground, getting a pair of size 13 shoes kicked deep up his ass, the color, race or sex of his help is not relevant or important. What is relevant is how fast the help arrives. When a cop is in a fight that he knows he's gonna lose, he wants help.

Eventually, a police officer will meet his match one day. I know. It was September 16, 1988 when that fact was made crystal clear to me. I had only one in my career and I still remember the dude's name. He had just been released from Stateville Penitentiary. Ladies and gentlemen. In this corner, the champion. Donnell Nolan

I was working the day shift when I got a radio dispatch: "Aggravated assault. Man with a gun." My back up was Officer Randy Holcomb. Randy had more time on the job than me. Randy wasn't no punk either. Randy stood a good 6' 3", 210 lbs. I was 6' 2", 155 lbs. Donnell was only 5' 8", 190lbs. All muscle. Penitentiary build. Plus, he didn't give a fuck about "the police."

The victim said that during an argument, Donnell pulled out a gun and threatened to shoot him. We had the victim sign a complaint and went to get Donnell. I went to the front door and Randy went around back just in case Donnell tried to bail on us. I knocked on the front door and stated: "Police. Open the door or we'll knock the door down." Donnell ran out the back door and walked into Randy, who was holding a .45 caliber semi auto in his hand. I made it around the back too. Now, here we were. Donnell, Randy and me. We were on the back porch, two stories high. I made my move.

I went to grab Donnell and found out immediately that that was a big mistake. His chest, back, and arm muscles were massive. Donnell grabbed me, picked my skinny ass up and threw me against a brick wall. Now, Randy jumps in. We tried to get him on the ground. Donnell was having fun throwing us around. I thank God he wasn't trying to hurt us. He was just proving a point. Donnell was saying, "Officers. You motherfuckers can't do shit with me. You'd better call for some help!" He was right. We had to.

Officers Marvin Dorsey and Mike Shields showed up to assist us. It took all four of us to get Donnell on the ground. Randy had to choke the shit out of him to make him stop fighting. Why did Donnell put up all that fight? Over a pack of cigarettes. Once we got him handcuffed and took him in (we never found his gun), I thanked him personally for not throwing me off that porch(he could have). Then I asked him, "How in the fuck did you get so strong?" Donnell said, "I just got out of Stateville. If you lift weights everyday for five years, you'll be strong too." We discussed his weightlifting regimen over a couple of Kool 100's. I provided the cigarettes. Free of charge

On a Personal Note

Racism and prejudice are touchy subjects. Especially to police officers. Some don't want to acknowledge it. But, it's always there. There is no way around it. In a better world, a policeman could be colorblind. We don't live in a better world. We live in the real world.

Have I seen White police officers treat Black and Hispanic offenders unfairly? Yes. Have I seen Black police officers treat White and Asian offenders unfairly? Yes. I was a police officer for 24 years and I've seen it all. Now, did I report what I saw to a supervisor? No. Why not? In Chapter 2, I mentioned that I was a patrolman and my badge was the same size as the patrolman standing next to me. I did not judge another officer's style of policing. Plus, I wasn't no angel out there myself. The "game" is the "game." In police work, you play the game for keeps and it does get ugly down in the trenches. Gang bangers ain't church deacons.

It's not about your color. It's about your conscience. Your mindset. How far is a policeman willing to go to accomplish the mission. Right or wrong. It's how an officer plays the "game" that matters in the end. Whichever way that officer chooses to play, he has to live with his decision.

Before I was a policeman, I was a black man. With that in mind, during my career, I had to pick a side. When I put my uniform on, I was The Police. When the police radio started blaring and those blue lights turned on, all the bullshit goes out the window. That was not the time to be thinking about color of skin. At those moments, the only colors that mattered were blue and white. The only thing that mattered was that I was on the side of right.

When I took my uniform off, I became a black man. A black husband. A father of black children. I lived in a black community. I know what's going on out there in the hood. I was an eyewitness to the plight of black men and women, black boys and girls who are marked for death, unemployment, substance abuse and incarceration by an America that doesn't give a damn about them. I know that D.W.B. (Driving While Black) does exist. Hell, I know that W.W.B. (Walking While Black) does exist. I decided early in my career that I was not gonna be the enemy of the black man. I was not going to persecute him, only prosecute him. That way, I could look at myself in the mirror and live with what I saw looking back at me.

In 1987, I was a recruit training in the 5th District. I remember working with an old timer who was about to retire. He was a brother. He gave me a great piece of advise about being the "black police." "Listen to me young man. As you go through your career, you're gonna see a few of your fellow officers do some fucked up shit to people that are a different race than they are. They can do it because when they end their tour of duty, they're gonna get in their cars and drive home to White, Hispanic or Asian neighborhoods. What neighborhood will you be driving home to? If you go out on these streets and treat people the right way, they won't forget it. If you fuck them over, they won't forget that either. They'll be the same people that you see walking down the block you live on. While you're with your wife, your kids and your dog. Now, they know where you live." I never forgot that advice.

CHAPTER 9

The Transformation From Civilian To Police Officer

(21 Essays)

"For those regarded as warriors . . . When engaged in battle . . .

The vanquishing of thine enemy can be the warriors only concern . . .

Suppress all human emotion and compassion . . . Kill whoever stands in thy way even if it be Lord God or Buddha himself . . . This truth lies at the heart of combat." (A quote from the movie "Kill Bill. Vol 1.")

Essay 1

I found out my first night on the streets just how good and how bad police work can be. It was the night of January 15, 1987. I met my FTO Donald Fanelli. We hit the streets and the first call we got was an "auto theft in progress." As we approached the address, we saw the car being driven away. Don hit the blue lights and the car pulled over. The driver just surrendered. The car's steering column was peeled, a screwdriver was on the floor and the rear vent window was smashed out. This was the first arrest of my career: Possession of Stolen Motor

Vehicle. Don told me right then, "We got lucky. All of the arrest we make won't be this easy."

About an hour later while in the station processing our arrestee, we heard a police chase on the radio involving other officers from the district. The offenders were driving at a high rate of speed to escape and a district car was in pursuit. At the corner of 103rd and King Drive, the fleeing vehicle went full speed through a red light. When the pursuing squad car followed through the red light, it crashed into a car broadside that had the right of way. Both of the passengers in that car were killed and the officers were seriously injured. And, the bad guys got away. As I listened to the tragic news, Don looked at me and said, "I told you so."

Essay 2

A police officer is like a defensive linesman on a football team. His job is to "try" and keep the "undesirable ones" out of the end zones of the "chosen ones." When the undesirables get into the end zone, it's a crime. When the policeman stops them, it's an arrest. To a police officer, it's a job, but it plays like a game. The hard part of the game is the policeman is easy to pick out of the crowd. The undesirables are not. The officer has to wait for them to make a move and react to it. Even a criminal has civil rights.

Who are the "chosen ones?" The happy, wholesome people. The people who do honest work, pay their taxes, raise their families and wouldn't hurt a fly. They are law abiding citizens that commit crimes. Petty crimes. Park on a fire hydrant. Run a stop sign. Smoke a little reefer to unwind. Nothing major.

They have good jobs, good credit, are carefree, happy, and they're gonna wear those damn flip flop sandals in the summer. They love taking pictures showing all their pearly white teeth and they just adore doggies and kitty cats. In short, they are sheep just waiting to be slaughtered by the wolves in society that prey on them. The "chosen ones" don't want to deal with the "undesirable ones." They do want protection from them. So, they created the police department.

What and where are the "end zones?" It could be anywhere. Your home. Your car. Your place of business or just walking down the street to the corner grocery store. There is no hiding place from the wolf. If you have what the wolf wants, it doesn't matter where you're at. To the wolf, it's only about one thing. Opportunity. Give a wolf an opportunity? Touchdown.

Essay 3

The beat cop is a part of the neighborhood. Like the corner grocery store. The officer is like an actor auditioning for a role in a movie. The neighborhood will determine what role the beat cop must play. If an officer wants to land the role, he has to sell himself to the community. At first, the people he sees on the beat are just faces in the crowd. As time goes by, the people become personalities to the beat cop. The same is true of the people's perception of the beat cop. They will either like the cop or they won't. If the people like him, his job will be easy. If they don't, he'll have to work harder. He won't get any cooperation and will have to fight for everything he gets.

All human beings by nature have a certain goodness instilled in them. There are a few misfits and that's job security for a police officer. There's always gonna be the need for the police. The impression a beat cop makes in the community will be his reputation. It would be in the best interest of the officer to make a good first impression. He won't get a second chance. There is a fine line that the cop must draw in the sand. Let the people know up front, "I provide a service to the community. If you cross the line, that service will require me to lock you up." If he let's the people know where he stands, there won't be any hard feelings. There is nothing better than a good understanding.

Essay 4

Ask yourself this question. What is more important to you? Your civil rights or your right to live in peace without fear. A police officer is given the mission to protect life and property. The officer is given a grocery list of rules, regulations, Department General Orders, codes of conduct, use of force models and constitutional laws to accomplish the mission. So now, the officer goes out on the streets to engage an enemy that has no rules to follow. The policeman is expected to win. How can anyone walk into an environment that is dirty, filthy and bloody; wearing a white suit and not expect to get any blood or dirt on him? He can't.

Police work is in many ways like an athletic contest. Take a look at the game of basketball. It's the police vs the crooks. They are trying to beat each other. The game is refereed by the public, the media, the Internal Affairs Division, the Police Review Board and the department. These groups only call fouls on the police officer. When you play basketball and all the fouls are getting called against you, you can't compete. You'll foul out of the game. The only way to stay in a game like this is to play more passively. And, you will lose the game. In basketball, it's only a game you've lost. In police work, playing passively can cost a police officer his life.

On the streets, it's a dog-eat-dog mentality. To survive the streets, you have to adapt the same mentality. It may cost the good citizens a few of their civil rights. However, it will make their police officers feel that they can compete. The more restraints that are placed on policemen will ultimately result in a more restrained and tentative police department. Who would benefit? The crooks. Who would suffer? The public.

(On a personal note: I've played basketball my whole life. Always wanted to play Isiah Thomas one on one. He was the best "little man" in the NBA during his time, he was my age and my size. Isiah would beat the dog shit out of me if we played a game with rules. If I could cheat and he had to play by the rules, I think I could beat him. Police officers that win the game sometimes have to cheat. They wouldn't win a game with no rules using a rulebook. In my career, I only cheated one time. All my other arrests were by the book. How did I cheat? I lied. In court. Under oath. Why did I cheat? I wanted to win. (P.S. The crook lied first. When the judge asked him, "How do you plea," he said, "Not guilty.")

Essay 5

Penitentiaries are full of convicts that share something in common. 40% of them are "dumb." 40% of them are "stupid." 20% are victims of bad circumstances. There is a difference. You want proof? Webster defines "dumb" as: Taking another man's life because you find out he's fucking your wife. Killing the man didn't change the fact that he was fucking your wife. Now, you're doing hard time for life. Guess what your wife is doing? She's getting fucked by her new man. Now, here comes "stupid." This is a true story. In Chicago, a group of armed men walked into an auto mechanic shop to commit a robbery. The mechanics told them that the owner was not in and the money was locked up. Come back in an hour. Those "stupid" fools left and came back an hour later. Now, the mechanics had CPD badges and 9mm.'s. Dumb and stupid go to prison. The smart criminals go to the White House, United States Senate, House of Representatives and City Hall.

What is the definition of a criminal? Someone that makes money and doesn't pay taxes on it. Who is worst? A poor, uneducated drug dealer trying to make a buck or a C.E.O. with a seven figure salary who turns to crime because he wants more money? Look at the prison time they get and you'll see who the American legal system thinks is worst. What is the definition of organized crime? The Mafia? Drug cartels? Street gangs? What about the United States government? The greatest violators of Commandment 17. Politicians tell the people anything to get elected. They talk about what the want to do for the American people. They don't talk about which ones.

The men and women who run this country have sold out for the almighty dollar. This includes federal, state and local government. If you throw "big business" in the picture, they all sleep in the same bed. The government talks about drugs are destroying the country. Cigarettes, alcohol, prescription drugs and guns are sold legally with the government's blessings and a government seal. They all kill people and destroy lives. But, they do make money.

The policy makers think that four letter words will improve the ills of the country. Jail (Build more). Guns (Buy more, or don't own any). Laws (Pass more). Cops (Hire more). Here's a four letter word for their ass. Jobs. When I was growing up, "Made in the USA" used to mean something. The factories, steel mills and manufacturing plants of yesteryear are all gone.

To get a job nowadays, you'll need a college degree and experience. Technology has replaced labor and people ask, "Why are Americans overweight?" To find a job making shoes, clothes, electronics, damn near everything, you have to fly to Asia. Slavery is alive and well in Asia. The sweatshop has replaced the plantation. Manufacture the merchandise over there (cheaply) and sell it all over the world. Simple economics. In some communities, the only job you can get is drug dealing. You don't need a degree or a hook-up. Only a desire to work. A man or women that just finished working a double shift at a steel mill is too tired to be on a street corner selling crack cocaine or selling pussy.

(On a personal note: Toward the end of my career, I enjoyed my job less. I felt like a tool being used by "the establishment" to oppress the people left by the wayside. I knew I was lucky. I had a job. I was just a pawn on the CPD. Just one fuck up away from being just like the people I was locking up. As a rookie, I took pride in making arrests. Later on, I started to ask myself, "What else has society left for these people as an alternative to crime?" Who was I locking up anyway? Nine times out of ten, it was a "brother." There was one positive point in locking up these young brothers. Only one. They got to see that this shit is for real. Talk is cheap. Telling them that they'll do time is one thing. Hearing the jury's verdict and hearing the judge's sentence brings the reality home. Hopefully, they get a short sentence. They're still young and they may be able to turn their lives around.)

Essay 6

There are some police officers that don't know how to talk to people and there are some that don't know how to treat people. Officers should always start the police/citizen interaction in a professional manner (Just remember that there are Five People. Handle accordingly). They will insult, belittle and disrespect citizens on the street. When the citizen being disrespected tells the officer: "Go fuck yourself," the officer gets angry. The reason that some people hate the police is caused, in some ways, by the police themselves. Abuse of the authority given them breeds contempt and cast a negative reflection on all police officers. There are some assholes out there serving and protecting. (Note: I'm not judging them. I just call 'em like I see 'em.) They make the job harder than it has to be.

The insult I heard most often was when an officer would tell a citizen, "Shut the fuck up!" The fact that he is a police officer does not give him the right to tell people when they can or can't talk. I've seen rookies, fresh out of college, telling 20, 30, even 40 year old men to shut up. Sometimes, they did it while they were standing inside the man's house! Do you know what you just did, dumb ass? You just challenged his manhood. Now, he could give less than a damn about this police/

citizen interaction. He wants to deal with this young motherfucker, standing in the place where he pays the rent, telling him when he can or can't talk. Officer, he wants to beat your ass!

Taking your squad car and blocking the whole street for no reason is just plain arrogant. People in their cars have places to go, people to see and things to do. Park your damn car, officer! Sometimes, an officer has been on the job too long or he ain't been on the job long enough.

The worst mistake a police officer can make is to give the impression that he doesn't care about the people he serves. (Note: Caring is not a job requirement. Cops don't have to let the public know that.) Even if he doesn't care, he should act like he does in public. At no scene is this more true than at the scene of a homicide. To a policeman, that man dead on the street may be a gang member. To the 10, 20, or 50 people on the scene screaming, crying and falling down on their knees, that man was a son, father, husband, brother and friend to them. Act like you don't care and that crowd is gonna see it. The person who killed him is gone. The rage in that crowd is at a fever pitch. These people want to fuck somebody up and they want to fuck somebody up right now. Who's there that they don't like? It would be in the best interest of any officer at the scene not to say or do anything to incite that crowd.

A cop only has a 33% chance to ever make an arrest. He will arrive at the scene of a crime too late, too early or right on time. A thief caught in the act knows he's going to jail. As the arresting officer, your job is to take him in. Be professional. It's not a sign of weakness to be polite. (He didn't steal anything from you, officer.) Be a prosecutor, not a persecutor. If the prisoner isn't giving the officer a hard time, don't give the prisoner one. Don't belittle him and ask a lot of irrelevant questions. (Trust me. He really doesn't feel like talking right now anyway.) Treat him with respect.

On a personal note

There were times that I could have arrested people and I choose to let some things slide, for my own personal reasons. Once, I got slapped in the face while on duty, in full uniform, in front of 20 witnesses. It was a traffic accident. The driver had crashed into a tree, totaling her car. She was white, drunk as hell and she weighed about 110lbs with her shoes on. If it had been a man, I probably would have taken my baton and beat on him like a set of drums. A policeman gets no cool points for beating up the weak. He'll get more respect from the public if he doesn't beat them up. The public is watching him. Beat up the weak and he'll get a bad label on the streets. The word will get out. (Note: She slapped me so I had to do something.)

I grabbed her little skinny ass, picked her up, carried her to a tree and cuffed her there ("That's hot!!"). That got me a bunch of cool points from the crowd. It was the talk of 47th st for days. When the people saw me back on the beat, they talked about how cool I handled the situation. I got respect.

In my career, I received 1 Department Commendation, 1 Special Commendation, 1 Above and Beyond trophy, 3 Complimentary Letters, 2 Fitness awards and over 40 Honorable Mentions. Those awards came from the Chicago Police Department. The greatest compliment an officer gets from the streets is, "Hey y'all. That officer's cool." If the officer can get that from the people that hate the police, then he's doing something right.

Essay 7

Law enforcement went through many changes during my years on the force. In 1986, the Chicago Police Department and the citizens of the City of Chicago had an understanding. The police officers served the public. But, we didn't live together. The public was over there and the police were over here. We came together when someone called 911. In the 1990's, along came community policing (C.A.P.S.). A good idea in theory. The police and the community working together. There would be monthly meetings where the police and the public would discuss concerns in the neighborhood. The people that attended the meetings were not the problem in the community. The problem was that the public was not made aware that for this to work, they would have to become more involved. They would have to become snitches. What happens to snitches in "the hood"? Snitches get stitches.

Who calls 911 the most? The anonymous citizen. Mr and Mrs. Unknown.

They have plenty to complain about. Their involvement is limited to calling 911. They will not identify themselves when they call. The anonymous citizen just wants the problem to go away. You can't really blame the public for not getting personally involved in criminal matters. Criminals carry guns and talking to the police will make those criminals turn those guns on those doing the talking. The State's Attorneys and

Mayors of America say that the public should cooperate with the police, come forward and get involved with prosecuting criminals. They can talk about snitching. Here's why.

Those same State's Attorneys and mayors have security details assigned to them. 24 hours a day. 7 days a week. It's easy to go to court and testify against hardcore gang members when you have armed security in front, in back, and on both sides of you. When you are standing all alone with a group of murderers looking to shut you up, it's a lot harder to be brave. Until the public is willing to come forward and stop hiding behind a telephone, there's only so much the police can do.

Essay 8

Gang members are feared in society because they can do whatever they want to do. The only laws they respect are their own street laws. If they decide someone needs a "beat down," they give them one. If they decide someone needs to die, he's dead. A long time ago, the most feared gang in Chicago was the Chicago Police Department. Now, the CPD is only the most organized gang. Fear is a powerful weapon. The police used to be feared in Chicago because it was a known fact what would happen if you challenged the CPD. In the 1980's, a wanted suspect would rather turn himself in to ABC news reporter Russ Ewing before he'd surrender to the CPD.

Back in my rookie days, there was an old saying that my mentor Herb taught me: "Two things in this world don't live long. Dogs that chase cars and people that fuck with the police." If you fought the police in the 1980's, you went to jail, but you went to the hospital first. That was understood. The police would let you experience the "serve" side of "serve and protect" and they didn't try to hide this fact from the public. The police wanted to send a clear message. If you don't fight: We Serve and Protect. If you do fight, the official policy of the street police: We Kick Ass and Take Names.

An unarmed citizen will talk plenty shit to an armed police officer. You best believe they won't talk that way to a Gangster Disciple with a 9mm. in his hand. A gangbanger can shoot someone in front of twenty witnesses and nobody saw nothing. At a police shooting, there will be witnesses lining up around the block waiting to tell the media what they saw the police officer do. Now, who's the baddest gang on the streets? The gangs are. The public gave the power to the same people who are terrorizing their communities and murdering their children. When the shit goes down, what does the community ask? "Where the police at?"

Essay 9

They don't make men like they used to. I was born in 1961, before all the gangs, Glocks and crack rocks. Growing up on the south side of the city, I had my fair share of fights. Back then, when I fought, I fought with my fist. And, I fought straight up: one on one. If I lost a fight, I learn something. I learned to leave whoever beat my ass alone. I didn't need a gun for protection and I didn't have to worry about getting shot the next day. Or, shot the same day. Stand up and fight like a man? That went out of style with bell bottoms, the afro pick, and platform shoes with horseshoe taps.

The children of the 80's and 90's don't fight like I did. They can't take their whipping like a man. Beat them up and they're coming back with a gun or 10 of their boys. Children from my era grew up watching Muhammad Ali fight Joe Frazier. These "new jacks" got Master P. and Jay Z. We had Sugar Ray Leonard and Tommy Hearns. They have Dr. Dre and Snoop Dogg.

In my teen years, I took up boxing. I learned something from the experience that helped me when I joined the police force. Everybody looks like they can fight when they get in the boxing ring. It's only after that bell rings that they find out how good they are.

Essay 10

The police uphold the law. The same laws hold up the police. An officer will be held accountable for every ticket, punch, kick, baton strike and bullet. I.A.D, the Police Review Board and the department heads all make decisions on incidents involving police officers that they didn't witness. How can anyone make a fair decision on a fight that they did not see? When a police officer gets penalized for fighting by the same people that sent him out to fight, what do you think the next policeman watching will do when it's his turn to fight? He won't show up. He'd be a fool to show up.

What does a police department stand to lose if an officer is K.I.A? Nothing. That dead officer can be replaced by a recruit in the police academy. When crack cocaine hit the streets of Chicago, crime began to skyrocket. In the late 80's and early 90's, homicides in the city began to reach near record numbers.

The CPD was out there, getting paid on the 1st and the 16th, putting in work. The blame for the increase in crime was placed, appropriately, on the problem. Gangs, guns and drugs. The police department was the solution to the problem and the police officers were left alone to deal with it.

By 2005, all major crimes, including homicides and shootings, were at record low numbers. Yet, the CPD was getting bad ink in the press. News flash. Police officers read the newspaper too. Here's another old saying in law enforcement: "You can't get in trouble if you don't do shit." There comes a time when the public that the police serve has to make a decision and pick a side. Who's gonna run the streets? The gangs, the public or the police? You either lead, you follow or you get the hell out the way.

Essay 11

The first law of nature is self preservation. Most cops don't want to fight. There are some that don't mind. Police officers didn't join the force to beat up people and they didn't join the force to get beat up either. The police want to use reason because they have too much to lose. Even if they win the fight, they may lose the battle in a courtroom.

A man and a woman will always remember their first love. A rookie police officer will always remember the first time he meets The Real Police. For me, it was when I met Officer Walter Boddie. He was a bad motherfucker. Walter was cool, calm, and the most professional police officer I had ever met. However, if you fucked with him, you'd better have your HMO insurance paid up.

If I had an arrestee that wouldn't go to jail without a fight, I would use one of Walter's lines as a way of reasoning. Then, I would add one of my own lines. (Walter's line: "I didn't come here to fight, sir. If you start fighting, I will try to catch up." My line: "This ain't got to go where you're taking it. If you take it there, you can't take it back.")

Police officers getting hurt or killed is bad for business. Policemen hurting or killing people who need hurting and killing is good for business. That sounds cold blooded, but it's true. Officers with years on the job don't want to do much police work. They want to come to work, keep the peace and go home in one piece. A criminal has only one thing to consider. What actions am I willing to take to get away with my crime? A cop must respond to that action. And, it better be the right response or here they come.

Essay12

For the most part, police work is boring and routine. Here you are, in a car, driving around with nowhere to go in particular when all of a sudden: Bang! Bang! Bang! Just like that. You go from 0 to 65 miles an hour. Adrenaline flowing and your heart's beating out your chest. There will be no advance warning when you have to heat up. Heat creates steam. Steam creates pressure. How do you release the pressure? A police officer needs to find a healthy way to release it.

Alcohol consumption was a common stress releaser amongst police officers. I know from personal experience (I used to drink everything on the bar). A policeman will lose his job if he smokes a little marijuana. He can be an alcoholic and become the Superintendent of Police.

Many officers (myself included) have "battled with the bottle." After our shift, the fellas and I would meet "down in the hole" and drink. Unlike John Q Public, police bars didn't have "last call for alcohol." On the afternoon shift, we shut down bars. On the midnight shift, we opened them. I had it bad for many years.

Whenever I was called downtown for a random drug test, I told my C/O the truth. "Sir. I ain't no dope fiend. I'm an alcoholic." A police officer that tries to drink the pressure of the job away just added more pressure to his life. I know. I've been there.

Essay 13

There are many police officers that are borderline insane and a few who are Section Eight. They're as prone to violence as the most hardened criminal on the streets. The most dangerous police officer is the cop that's close to retirement. He/She is older, slower, and they don't fight as well as they used to. But, I'll be damned if they plan on losing a fight. They will shoot your ass dead! Almost at the end and here you come fucking with them. To a seasoned veteran, making an arrest is the farthest thing from his mind. Been there. Done that. He can take it or leave it. Make a veteran officer feel that you're trying to deny him of his pension and retirement and you just turned that veteran into someone with serious thoughts of murder on his mind.

Early in my career, I learned this fact about people. Nobody wants to be in the company of a crazy person. You don't have to really be crazy. An officer that can fake being crazy will not get challenged as much as Officer "Friendly." On the streets, the only officer that some people will comply to is Officer "Crazy." Try to act like a gentleman and the people will call you a "goofy." Barney Fife. Take out your gun, walk toward a crowd with murder in your eyes, promise to kill the first SOB that gives you any shit and watch the crowd disperse. Is it professional? Does it work?

Essay 14

Mental health is just as important as physical health. If he's not careful, a police officer can have a mental breakdown. Guns, drugs, armed robberies, beatings, stabbings, shootings, rape, innocent victims, blood, murder and death. There will be days that a policeman just doesn't feel like dealing with the shit. A cop has life issues to deal with too. His wife is on drugs, his kids are failing in school, his car won't start, his mother's dying from cancer and he needs to make more money. There will be good days and bad days. The suicide rate in law enforcement is high for a reason.

My own transformation from civilian to police officer was progressive from year to year. I got progressively worst. Years 1-5, I prayed a simple prayer: "Lord, don't let me get killed." Years 5-10, my prayer changed: "Lord, if I must die, let me take a few with me." Years 10-15, I stopped praying: "I wish a motherfucker would try to do something to me!" Years 15-20: "Come on, pull your gun out. My kid's are already grown." Year 20, I became more at peace: "Sir, how are you today. Why don't you just leave me alone. If not, I'm not gonna do anything to you right now. I'm gonna find all the people that you love the most in life and kill them first. Then, I'm gonna kill you." If you cross the line with a cop that's this close to "pop goes the weasel," you might get a plunger shoved up your ass.

As a public servant, police officers must keep their inner turmoil away from their professional life. It's not easy. The more they see, the more numb they become and the less humane they become. They don't see people as people anymore. People are placed in categories ranging from those I need to help to those I need to kill. The penitentiary and the graveyard are the only suitable places for some members of society. I knew it was getting to be retirement time when I started having dreams about meeting one of them in the flesh. Bang! Bang! Bang! Bang! Bang! Bang! "You picked the wrong nigger to fuck with, junior. Rest in peace."

Essay 15

The use of deadly force is the biggest decision a police officer will ever have to make. When to shoot and when not to shoot. A split second decision that can have lifelong repercussions. Cops don't meet many people that deserve a death sentence. Most people are ordinary, good natured human beings. However, police officers can't tell that just by looking at them. Some officers are good. Not that good.

The public is under the false impression that they do not have to obey a policeman's order if they didn't do anything wrong. Let's say, for instance, you just walked out of your house. You know this. The police officer doesn't know. What you don't know is thirty minutes ago, your neighbor down the block just got robbed at gun point. The police officer knows. Now, the cop sees you and walks up to you, telling you to take your hands out of your pocket. You refuse because: 1. "I ain't done nothing." 2. "I don't like the police." What you're doing right now is making that officer nervous. Policemen don't have a very trusting nature to begin with. People lie to the police all the time. Sometimes, even when they don't need to lie.

I was lucky in that I never had to pull my trigger. That's not to say I never drew my weapon, I pulled it out many, many times. What can a citizen do to make a policeman pull his weapon out? Try these simple steps: Refuse to show your hands on demand. Open your car door on a traffic stop. Reach under your car seat on a traffic stop. Have any kind of object in your hand. Reach inside your pants or coat pockets. Fail to follow verbal commands. Start to crowd in on a cop and he tells you to back off. If you did those things to me, I'd pull my weapon. If you didn't stop doing those things, I'd pull my trigger. The fastest draw is not from the holster. The fastest draw is my gun in my hand.

I still see the corner where I did almost shoot a man. 43rd st and Berkeley. I was with my partner Freddie. We were on patrol and got flagged down at 43rd and Cottage Grove. The man who stopped us said this "young boy" just pulled a gun on him, aimed it in his face and walked away down 43rd St. We figured that he was long gone by now. What the hell. Tell us what he looked like and we'll look for him. We drove down 43rd St and at Berkeley, there he was. Freddie and I stepped to him. What we didn't know was the gun he had wasn't real. It looked real, but it was a toy. That stupid bastard, instead of telling us the gun wasn't real, started reaching in his pocket to show us. Freddie and I both pulled our guns out and aimed down on him. He screams,

"It ain't real!!" We arrested him on a city charge. Replica of a firearm. There was no charge on the books for being a stupid fool.

A lot of people are against the death penalty. I spent 24 years with the death penalty inches away from my right hand. The Chicago Police Department issued .38 caliber +P ammo to old timers like Herb, Freddie and me. We carried .357 magnums. (John Williams, my other partner, carried a 9mm.) I took that department shit and put it in my locker. I loaded my .357 magnum with .357 ammunition. I wasn't looking for trouble. But, if I was going to face the "ultimate test," I wasn't trying to score a C+. I wanted to score an A+in the use of deadly force.

Essay 16

The police department is a business. The officers I worked with were like family. My partners were even closer than that. They're like my blood relatives. Herb, Freddie, John and Mike were like Kenneth, Rodney and Everett, the three brothers I lost in my life. We were together through the good, the bad and the ugly. When an officer I work with is hurt or killed, it's like a bad dream. Sadly, I have experienced that nightmare twice in my career. Two officers I worked with were gunned down by handguns. One officer lived. The other officer died. Now, I took it personal.

If any offender shoots my partner in front of me, I hope that he understands that today is his lucky day. I won't be taking him to jail. He won't have to worry about a court date, raising bond or hiring a lawyer because I will be holding court right here on the streets. Right now. Court is in session and there will be no recess. The final verdict is this. If he doesn't kill me, I'm killing him. There is nothing to talk about. He took it there. He can't take it back.

Essay 17

The crimes that will affect a policeman the most are the crimes that don't make sense. Death, pain and suffering are things that a cop gets used to seeing. Some people are going to die just from the choices they make in life. Gang bangers die. Drug addicts die. Soldiers die. Police officers die. It goes with the territory. Why do young kids riding their bikes have to die in drive-by shootings? Why do teenage boys with Air Jordans on their feet get robbed and killed for their shoes?

A cop gets to see up close the wretchedness of the human race. Think about the crimes you read about in the paper or see on the evening news. You read it and see it and you're in shock. You can turn the page or change the channel. Not the police officer. He has to see it. Smell it. Hear the high pitched scream of a mother who's just had her son murdered. Tell a father to come to the hospital because his ten year old daughter has been gang raped. A cop sees the victim of these horrible crimes and knows that the man or woman that did it is still out there. A low down dog who will do it again. And again.

Essay 18

There will be many times in every cop's career where he will see something done to a victim that he will take very personal. I have had many of those days etched in my memory. One in particular, I will share with you.

I was assigned a "battery victim" at Mercy Hospital. Nothing new about a battery victim. Happens all the time. When I got to the hospital, I saw the victim's clothes and I knew that this was much more than just a bloody nose. There was blood everywhere. He was bleeding so profusely that I had to wait for the ER staff to stop the bleeding before I could even talk to him. When I finally talked to him, he related the following.

The man went to the Stateway Garden Projects to visit his sickly mother. As he attempted to enter the building, he was stopped by the drug dealers that sold drugs out of the building. They wanted to search him. He told them why he was there and that he was not trying to infiltrate their drug operation. He only wanted to see his mother. When he would not allow them to search him, 4-8 gang members, some with baseball bats, knocked him down and proceeded to beat the living shit out of him.

Both of his arms were broken, his ribs were broken, his skull was split wide open and teeth were knocked out his mouth. When the police began responding to the 911 call, those cowards ran back in the building. The man wanted to see his mother and almost died because of it. Against this helpless man, those punks were so hard. Why did they scatter like roaches when the police arrived? Because, that's what rats and roaches do when you shine a light on them.

I really wanted to go to that building with a machine gun and shoot the first motherfucker that tried to search me. I'm talking about going Charles Bronson on that ass! Gangbangers are real tough when they're dealing the cards. I wanted to deal the cards to them and see how they like it. When a police officer begins to turn into the thing that he hates the most, it's time to do something else with his life. At that point in his life, it's time to retire.

Essay 19

In my career, I made lots of arrests. The one I'm most proud of was the one I didn't make. As my mentor Herb told me on many occasions, "Throw him back in the water, T-Man. We'll let this one live." The year was 2001. The Marlo case. But first, I need to take the reader back in time to 1992.

The all time record for homicides in one calendar year in the City of Chicago is 970 murders. That was in 1974. In 1992, the number of homicides were in the 900's with weeks to go until 1993. I was at 26th and California, the criminal court building, waiting for a court case that I was the arresting officer on. I overheard a State's Attorney talking to another State's Attorney about the growing homicides in the city. He said, "Boy, homicides sure are rising. I hope we break the record." I wanted to shoot him in the back of his head. Bang!! Bang!! "Are you happy now? That's one more, asshole!!"

Why do you think an Illinois State's Attorney would say some shit like that? Here's what I think: 1. He was white. He probably didn't live in Chicago. Neither did his family or friends. 2. Who was being murdered? Blacks and Hispanics. 3. He only saw those homicides as cases he could win in court and further his career. Damn the victim of the crime. Now, fast forward to 2001.

On that night in 2001, I was working with my partner John and we observed a group of young teenagers out pass their curfew. Curfew citations are like gold to an officer assigned to the midnight watch. I looked at John and said, "Well Po' Pimp, it looks like we're through for the night." Six curfews are a good night's work. We stopped them, found out that five were underage and prepared to take them home. A young female officer, Alise Howell, came by to assist us with the female juveniles. Police officers search everybody before putting them into a squad car. We asked all of them, "Do you have anything on you that you're not supposed to have?" They all said no. Alise calls me over and says, "T. I think that boy has something on him." It was Marlo. I searched him and found a .25 caliber semi auto pistol in his coat pocket. I called it in on the radio.

Once I called it in, it's on the tape and I can't make it go away. Once we got into the station, we learned the facts. These kids had been to the movies and when the movie ended, a gang fight broke out. During the confusion and fighting, a gun fell on the ground and Marlo picked it up. Marlo was 17 years old. My daughter was 17. Would my daughter pick up a free gun? Yes. Unlawful possession of a firearm is a felony. This young man was gonna be scarred for life. A convicted felon.

A month later, I'm in court for the probable cause hearing. This is the court hearing where the judge determines if the arresting officer (me) had probable cause to make the arrest. If so, the case gets transferred to the criminal courts building. If not, the case is dropped. Before court began, I went to check Marlo's "rap sheet" to see if he had any prior arrest. There were none. This was his first arrest. Then, in the hallway, I met his mother. She showed me awards that this boy received in school. This kid was very book smart. He just did something stupid. Like all kids do.

I went to talk to the State's Attorney assigned the case to see if he'd be willing to kick this down to a misdemeanor. I told him how he came to possess the gun. The attorney (Yep. He was white.) looked at Marlo's rap sheet, acknowledged that it was his first arrest and, without blinking an eye, looked me in my face and said, "Fuck him!" Then he turned and walked away. I had a flashback to 1992 and made up my mind right then. "You ain't gonna score no points on this brother." When that attorney asked me, under oath, to point to the man I recovered the gun from, I looked at Marlo and said, "That doesn't look like him." Just like that. Case dismissed.

Once the charges were dropped, I met Marlo outside as he walked out the courtroom a free man. I talked to him like a father would talk to his own child. I said, "I don't want to ever see you in a courtroom again, boy! As long as you are black, there may not always be a job waiting for you. There will always be a jail cell waiting for your black ass." That was my gift to the brothers. I cut one loose.

My FTO, Don Fanelli, told me the good things that come with being a cop. I can buy a home, a car, and take care of my family. Now, as the preliminary officer assigned to any case, that case is mine. I can drop a bomb on the people or I can cut them some slack. Don knew that so he told me. That State's Attorney didn't know that, but I showed him. Fuck Marlo? No. Fuck you!! This is my case. I didn't work for the State's Attorney. He worked for me.

Essay 20

The best feeling a police officer gets is when he draws up a plan, sets the trap, and catches the rat. It is at that supreme moment that he knows he is The Police. That's when the job becomes rewarding. At some point in a policeman's career, he begins to figure out what law enforcement is all about. Law enforcement is what it means to him. This is his life on the line. The police department, the media, the public and everything else becomes an afterthought. A police officer has to do the job his way. When a police officer is killed in action, what happens? There's a headline in the paper: "Officer killed." A few days later: "Officer laid to rest." What happens next? Officer forgotten.

There is nothing noble about dying in the line of duty. Where is the honor in a policeman losing his life trying to arrest a drug dealer? Or a car thief? Or some crack head committing a burglary? To lose his life to preserve another's life is honorable. I read a story about a soldier that threw his body on a live grenade to save the lives of his fellow soldiers. He died an honorable death. He was a true hero. John Q Public expects a police officer to risk his life chasing a pickpocket who stole their wallet with $5 dollars in it.

(On a (final) personal note: As a sworn police officer, I took an oath and I knew that in taking the oath, I would be taking some personal risk. But, to be completely honest, I want to tell the reader what I really feel about that stolen wallet. I would try to get your stolen property returned to you. However, if I thought I might lose my life in the attempt, I only have one thing to say. DAMN YOUR WALLET!! The same thing goes for your car, watch, big screen TV, fur coat, jewelry, money and everything else you own. Nothing that you own is worth me risking my life. The only reason I would risk my life is to save your life. You can buy a new wallet.)

Essay 21

I took the oath of office and was sworn in as an officer on November 21, 1986. I really don't remember what I swore to. I took another oath after five years on the force. That oath I remember. I said it over and over.

The Oath

"Heavenly father. I hear by swear and vow. That any man, woman, or child. Be they black, white, red, brown, yellow, pink or polka dot. Gay, lesbian, heterosexual, bisexual, or they're undecided right now. Be they deaf, drunk, dumb, cracked up, doped down, down with "King Hoover," blind, crippled or crazy. If you try to hurt me, I'm gonna do whatever I have to do to whip your ass. In Jesus name. Amen."

When I hit the streets, a police officer had a car, a radio, a cup of coffee, a pair of handcuffs, ticket books, a revolver and a baton. When I retire, there will be video cameras mounted on the windshields of squad cars, portable data terminals, GPS tracking devices in police vehicles, audio recording devices and "pod" cameras attached to street poles that are activated by the sound of gunfire. The technology may help the "new school" of police officers find the bad guy. Once they find him, they still have to answer the same questions us "old timers" had to answer. "What do I do now? Do I go get him or do I run home?"

ABOUT THE AUTHOR

Terrence Howard served as a patrolman with the Chicago Police Department for 24 years (September 8, 1986-June 22, 2010). He was assigned to the Prairie district (021) as a beat officer, plainclothes officer, desk officer, field training officer, acting desk sergeant and lock-up keeper at various times during his career. A lifelong resident of Chicago, he received numerous commendations, honorable mentions and fitness awards from the CPD during his tenure. He remained in his hometown after retirement.